ROUSSEAU—
TOTALITARIAN
OR LIBERAL?

Number 589
Columbia Studies in the Social Sciences
Edited by the Faculty of Political Science
of Columbia University

Rousseau—Totalitarian or Liberal?

By John W. Chapman

AMS PRESS
NEW YORK

THE COLUMBIA STUDIES IN THE SOCIAL SCIENCES (formerly the Studies in History, Economics, and Public Law) is a series edited by the Faculty of Political Science of Columbia University and published by Columbia University Press for the purpose of making available scholarly studies produced within the Faculty.

Reprinted with the permission of Columbia University Press
From the edition of 1956, New York
First AMS EDITION published 1968
Manufactured in the United States of America

Library of Congress Catalogue Card Number: 68-54260

AMS PRESS, INC.
New York, N.Y. 10003

For
Janet Goodrich
and
Hazel Perry Chapman

PREFACE

THIS IS NOT a book about Rousseau's influence, whether for good or evil, although that certainly has been great. Nor does it attempt to appraise his explanation of moral and political phenomena, important as that task may be. Rather its central aim is analysis of his political theory with a view to explaining the sense in which it deserves to be called liberal.

Rousseau's political theory is regarded widely as fundamentally totalitarian. It does contain illiberal elements. So do the works of others whose place in the development of liberal thought is secure. Yet Rousseau is given special responsibility for the emergence of totalitarianism. Indeed, the very scope of the indictment against him suggests not so much comprehension of his work as misunderstanding. Possibly another interpretation of his political theory may be entertained. He did not accept the notion, central to eighteenth-century French liberalism, of a historical harmony between man and his social environment. He would have thought inadequate the moral and psychological theories of the English utilitarians. Perhaps Rousseau's conception of man is closer to that of modern liberals than we have suspected. Concern with his work as a source of totalitarian doctrine may have obscured its contribution to the theory and practice of liberal democracy.

This book is divided into three parts, the first of which is an exposition of Rousseau's theory of human nature and dynamics. Part Two deals directly with his political theory and seeks to show its logical connections with his psychological and moral theories. Part Three undertakes to explain what is novel in his ideas about man and the state and to appraise their bearing for liberal doctrines. Throughout I try to indicate significant points of agreement and difference with other interpretations of his thought. It will be apparent to the reader that my debt to these is great.

I owe an intellectual debt of a more general nature to Professor Solomon E. Asch's *Social Psychology* and to Professor Richard B. Brandt's *Hopi Ethics: A Theoretical Analysis*. Both of these works aided me greatly in the task of formulating a systematic approach to Rousseau's psychological and moral ideas.

I have relied whenever possible upon accepted and easily available translations of Rousseau's writings. In cases where no translation has been made, I have translated the passage myself.

For their counsel I wish to thank Professor Robert M. MacIver and the late Professor Franz Neumann of Columbia University. I desire also to express my appreciation to Professor J. Roland Pennock of Swarthmore College for his exacting encouragement through the years. It was he who first introduced me to the study of Rousseau's writings and from him I caught the feeling that it was worth continuing.

JOHN W. CHAPMAN

Smith College
Northampton, Mass.
December, 1955

ACKNOWLEDGMENTS

THE AUTHOR IS grateful to E. P. Dutton and Co. for permission to quote extensively from Rousseau's *Social Contract and Discourses*, translated by G. D. H. Cole, and from his *Émile*, translated by Barbara Foxley.

The author is also grateful to the following publishers for permission to quote: Thomas Nelson and Sons, for Rousseau's *Considerations on the Government of Poland* and *Constitutional Project for Corsica*, in *Rousseau: Political Writings*, translated by Frederick Watkins; St. Martin's Press and Macmillan and Co., for the fourth edition of Bernard Bosanquet's *The Philosophical Theory of the State* and his *Psychology of the Moral Self*; Librairie Gallimard, for Bernard Groethuysen's *Jean-Jacques Rousseau;* and The Beacon Press, for *The Rise of Totalitarian Democracy*, by J. L. Talmon.

The Political Quarterly has kindly permitted me to quote from A. D. Lindsay's article, "The State in Recent Political Theory," which appeared in the first number of that journal.

Finally, I wish to thank the Aristotelian Society for permission to quote from A. D. Lindsay's contribution to the symposium on "Purpose and Mechanism," published in Vol. XII of *Proceedings of the Aristotelian Society*.

J. W. C.

CONTENTS

Part One

HUMAN NATURE AND DYNAMICS

Notre véritable étude est celle de la condition humaine. ÉMILE, BOOK I

Chapter

1

MAN
AND HIS
ENVIRONMENT

Rousseau's description of man's psychological capacities and moral potentialities is found mainly in his discussion of the "state of nature," or more exactly, in that stage of the "state of nature" in which men lived dispersed and "maintained no kind of intercourse with one another." [1] Here we find his ideas about our nature as it would be in a nonsocial environment.

He sees in man three distinct capacities and two potentialities. Man seeks his own welfare and has a need to preserve himself. In addition, he has an emotional capacity for sympathy, a tendency to respond to the needs of others which takes the form of negative reaction to pain. Thirdly, man has an understanding or cognitive ability. The potentialities distinguished are those for freedom and perfectibility.

Rousseau's view of the basic human endowment is summed up in the following passage:

Contemplating the first and most simple operations of the human soul, I think I can perceive in it two principles prior to reason, one of them deeply interesting us in our own welfare and preservation, and the other exciting a natural repugnance at seeing any other sensible being, and particularly any of our own species, suffer pain or death. It is from the agreement and com-

---

[1] Rousseau, *A Discourse on the Origin of Inequality*, in *The Social Contract and Discourses*, trans. G. D. H. Cole, p. 227. All references to this *Discourse* are to Cole's translation.

bination which the understanding is in a position to establish between these two principles, without its being necessary to introduce that of sociability, that all the rules of natural right appear to me to be derived.[2]

Man has an "understanding" but not "reason." He is compassionate but not endowed with a social instinct.

That man is unsociable does not imply he is either antagonistic toward his fellows or desirous of surpassing them. With specific reference to Hobbes' view of human nature, Rousseau says:

Egoism must not be confused with self-respect . . . . Self-respect is a natural feeling which leads every animal to look to its own preservation, and which, guided in man by reason and modified by compassion, creates humanity and virtue. Egoism is a purely relative and factitious feeling, which arises in the state of society.[3]

Man is neither sociable nor egoistic. These are both attitudes or sentiments which arise only in a social environment. In the "state of nature" he is a psychologically self-sufficient being, a solitary animal concerned mainly with gratification of immediate physical desires.

As to the connection between man's interest in his own welfare and his capacity for compassion, Rousseau is somewhat ambiguous. In the *Discourse on Inequality* he regards compassion as a distinct emotional capacity, whereas, in *Émile* it is seen as derivative from self-respect.[4] In *Inequality* Rousseau says it is "certain that compassion is a natural feeling"[5] and makes no mention of its root in man's love for himself. Rather, this feeling is seen as the foundation of conscience, "the cause of that repugnance, which

---

[2] *Ibid.*, p. 193.   [3] *Ibid.*, p. 223, n. 2.

[4] According to Robert Derathé, "Self-love being the only primitive impulse for him, Rousseau is under the obligation to attach the other natural impulses of man to it and to show how they derive from it. It is thus that in *Émile* compassion becomes a feeling derived from self-love while the second *Discourse* opposed the two principles to one another" (*Le Rationalisme de J.-J. Rousseau*, pp. 99-100). Author's translation.

[5] Rousseau, *Inequality*, p. 226.

every man would experience in doing evil, even independently of the maxims of education." [6] In *Émile,* Rousseau describes sympathy as the first relative sentiment that appears in man [7] and traces the beginnings of conscience to appearance of gratitude. Compassion does not arise until man becomes independent and conscious of his powers. Gratitude is seen as the necessary response to recognition of benevolent action. Both emotions have reference to the self. But Rousseau affirms that conscience functions in a disinterested fashion. Clearly he is thinking of a capacity to respond to the needs of others which is functionally different from, although it may have its origin in, self-respect. For this reason compassion is included in the list of man's basic capacities.

Man's cognitive ability is severely circumscribed. It is sufficiently powerful to produce consciousness of self, otherwise Rousseau could not speak of self-respect. Also this power can combine the dictates of self-love and sympathy so as to make man's behavior generally peaceful. These accomplishments mark the limits of human understanding. Man "can have neither foresight nor curiosity." [8] Indeed, this creature Rousseau describes hardly deserves to be called man, so restricted is his mental horizon. He has desires and emotions. But these function in so limited a cognitive context they cannot be described as human.

Man has, however, two potentialities which distinguish him from the other animals. He is "free" and "perfectible." What is the meaning of these terms? Man is free in that he is not governed entirely by impulse. "Nature lays her commands on every animal, and the brute obeys her voice. Man receives the same impulsion, but at the same time knows himself at liberty to acquiesce or resist." [9] He is conscious of alternatives and free to choose among them in a way that

6 *Ibid.,* p. 227.

7 Rousseau, *Émile,* trans. Barbara Foxley, p. 184. All references to *Émile* are to Foxley's translation.

8 Rousseau, *Inequality,* p. 211. 9 *Ibid.,* p. 208.

no other animal is.   Outside society this capacity for choice
remains undeveloped and has only immediate survival value.
Man is only potentially a self-determining being.

By "perfectibility" Rousseau means that man's capacities
are such that when fully developed he finds his greatest
satisfaction in values and actions pronounced right by reason
and conscience.   We have a "faculty of self-improvement,
which, by the help of circumstances, gradually develops all
the rest of our faculties." [10]   Although Rousseau here refers
to development of "all" man's faculties, his conception of
perfectibility should not be understood to mean either that
man is plastic with respect to values or that he acquires his
moral attitudes in an arbitrary fashion.   Rousseau does think
that in society man may acquire immoral attitudes, act on
bad motives, and pursue wrong values.   He even raises
doubts about man's capacity for moral action by suggesting
that he may be incapable of acting other than for his personal good.   But he believes also that there is a direction to
human development from which man may not deviate without violation of his moral potentialities and failure to
achieve maximum satisfaction.   There are attitudes and
values inherent in and appropriate to his nature.   But the
way to these depends on respect for the dynamics of that
nature.   In *Émile,* Rousseau says:

We are born sensitive and from our birth onwards we are
affected in various ways by our environment.   As soon as we
become conscious of our sensations we tend to seek or shun the
things that cause them, at first because they are pleasant or un-
pleasant, then because they suit us or not, and at last because
of judgments formed by means of the ideas of happiness and
goodness which reason gives us.   These tendencies gain strength
and permanence with the growth of reason, but hindered by our
habits they are more or less warped by our prejudices.   Before
this change they are what I call Nature within us.[11]

[10] *Ibid.,* pp. 208-9.   [11] Rousseau, *Émile,* p. 7.

For Rousseau perfectibility implies that man is not a dynamically empty creature. There is "Nature within us." We possess autonomous tendencies which have a definite pattern of development.[12] There is an inherent directedness to the growth of our capacities which we may either thwart or follow. Man either distorts or perfects himself. Through reason he acquires an idea of his perfection, of the obligations and values appropriate to his nature, and may, if he so chooses, shape himself in accordance with this knowledge.

Outside society man is a limited and peaceful animal living for himself and the day alone. He is self-conscious, self-seeking, self-sufficient, and capable of feeling compassion for his fellows when observed in pain. He has no time perspective, but he is not governed by instinct alone. He is free. Above all, he is capable of psychological and moral growth. What happens to man when he enters into enduring relations with his fellows? How is he altered by society?

Rousseau thinks man in the "state of nature" is in equilibrium with his environment. So long as his physical needs are easily met, his psychological capacities do not develop. "Everything seems to remove from savage man both the temptation and the means of changing his condition." [13] Initially man is an adaptive creature. Change in his surroundings sends him toward society. Population increases, climate becomes less favorable, food less plentiful, and the equilibrium of the "state of nature" is disrupted. Man finds it more difficult to satisfy his wants and in consequence is forced to think. Men learn sporadically to cooperate and finally stumble into society.

Two principles are involved in Rousseau's analysis of the transformation of man's nature as he moves from a natural

12 Bernard Groethuysen refers to a "légalité intérieure." *Jean-Jacques Rousseau,* ch. 1.

13 Rousseau, *Inequality,* p. 211.

to a social environment.   Increased difficulty of satisfying needs leads to enlargement of cognitive ability.   This, in turn, gives rise to new needs and emotions.   "The human understanding is greatly indebted to the passions, which . . . are also much indebted to the understanding." [14]   A reciprocal relation obtains between motivational and intellectual processes.   Pressure of wants develops man's mental powers, which react back upon and transform his wants.

In society man acquires use of his latent capacity to reason and becomes egoistic and materialistic.   He thinks about his fellows, calculates their behavior, and compares himself with them.   Mutual comparisons arouse selfish feelings, and men become dominated by *amour propre*.   "Instead of a being, acting constantly from fixed and invariable principles . . . we find in [him] only the frightful contrast of passion mistaking itself for reason, and of understanding grown delirious." [15]   Reason is corrupted by the very emotions and desires its development brought into existence.   Man is not only transformed but distorted by social life.   Once vanity arises he is faced with dissatisfaction.   He acquires more wants than he can gratify and desires to excel his fellows. "Self-love, which concerns itself only with ourselves, is content to satisfy our own needs; but selfishness, which is always comparing self with others, is never satisfied and never can be; for this feeling, which prefers ourselves to others, requires that they should prefer us to themselves, which is impossible." [16]   Selfishness makes man a creature very much like that described by Hobbes, one whose desires are insatiable and whose self-respect depends on the deference of others.

Selfishness precludes realization both of man's perfectibility and his capacity for self-determination.   "That man is truly free who desires what he is able to perform, and does what he desires." [17]   A person cannot be free if he strives for

[14] *Ibid.*, p. 210.   [15] *Ibid.*, p. 189.
[16] Rousseau, *Émile*, p. 174.   [17] *Ibid.*, p. 48.

goals only because others expect him to or in order to surpass them. Nor can he achieve perfection if he fails to be morally autonomous. True freedom requires independent determination and achievement of purposes.

Rousseau's view of the causes and consequences of egoism is central to his theory of human nature and appears in various forms throughout his writings. In the *Discourse on the Moral Effects of the Arts and Sciences* he says, "We no longer dare seem what we really are, but lie under a perpetual restraint." [18] In *Inequality* he argues that "social man constantly lives outside himself" and refers to "the indifference to good and evil which arises from this disposition." [19] In *The Social Contract* he deplores a materialistic scheme of values on the ground that "it sells the country to softness and vanity, and takes away from the State all its citizens, to make them slaves one to another, and one and all to public opinion." [20] Toward the close of his career, in *Rousseau, Judge of Jean-Jacques*, he asserts that "slaves and dupes of their self-love, men live not in order to live but to make others believe that they have lived!" [21] These passages suffice to show that failure to achieve autonomy is fundamental to Rousseau's diagnosis of moral failure and dissatisfaction. Man is prideful, consequently takes his attitudes and values from his group, and so does not realize his potentialities for moral freedom and goodness. Instead of forming their characters according to the dictates of reason and conscience, men become victims of one another's egoism. They lack both individuality and humanity.

Rousseau does not think domination by selfishness the necessary outcome of the expression of human tendencies in

18 Rousseau, *A Discourse on the Arts and Sciences*, in *The Social Contract and Discourses*, trans. G. D. H. Cole, p. 149. All references to this *Discourse* are to Cole's translation.

19 Rousseau, *Inequality*, pp. 270-71.

20 Rousseau, *The Social Contract*, trans. G. D. H. Cole, Book III, ch. 4. All references to *The Social Contract* are to Cole's translation.

21 Quoted by Ernst Cassirer, *The Question of Jean-Jacques Rousseau*, trans. Peter Gay, p. 51.

society.   This is the result of a defective environment, one
which disregards the autonomous tendencies in man's nature.
Along with his indictment of society there always goes in
Rousseau's work the reservation that men's condition is of
their own making and can be corrected.   At the conclusion
of the *Discourse on the Arts and Sciences,* he asserts that
moral improvement is within reach of all and urges men to
"listen to the voice of conscience, when the passions are
silent." [22]

The difficulty is that an inequalitarian and materialistic
society places men in a relation of conflict.   Society "necessarily leads men to hate each other in proportion as their
interests clash." [23]   But why do their interests clash?   Partly
because these are based on men's values, and men who value
wealth and superiority will have a hateful attitude toward
one another.   They have lost contact with their innermost
selves and have become power seekers.

Rousseau prescribes that man make his own appraisals of
values if he would discover those appropriate to his nature.
He must also abandon the quest for power.   "Power itself is
servile when it depends upon public opinion; for you are
dependent on the prejudices of others when you rule them by
means of those prejudices." [24]   Moral autonomy is the condition both of perfection and satisfaction.

But how can man listen to his conscience in society?   How
can he not be vain and incapable of using his reason to
evaluate values?   To discover how man may achieve moral
independence we must examine more closely Rousseau's view
of the relations between reason and emotion, and especially
that structure of emotions and attitudes called conscience.
This is the aim of the following chapter.

[22] Rousseau, *Arts and Sciences,* p. 174.
[23] Rousseau, *Inequality,* p. 274.   [24] Rousseau, *Émile,* p. 47.

Chapter

2

REASON
AND
CONSCIENCE

IN SOCIETY, Rousseau argues, men become vain and selfish. They acquire needs for approval and deference. In consequence they imitate and morally enslave one another. This is not the only way men may acquire goals and attitudes. These depend also on our understanding of human needs and relationships. Personal insight may displace mutual conditioning and influence in formation of men's ethical orientation. Conscience rather than prestige may become the decisive force in motivation. Rousseau describes how these changes in values, attitudes, and motives can be accomplished in terms of the education of Émile, the "natural man."

Rousseau's objective is cultivation of man's capacity to reason. By means of this power man appraises values correctly and acquires that structure of attitudes called conscience. "Reason alone teaches us to know good and evil. Therefore conscience, which makes us love the one and hate the other, though it is independent of reason, cannot develop without it." [1] Reason is crucial to the realization of man's moral potentialities.

At the outset we need to be aware of how Rousseau envisages the problem of human development and of the general nature of his solution to it. He sees man dependent

1 Rousseau, *Émile,* p. 34.

on society for full development of his capacities. But there is a sequence to this development according to which reason appears later than capacity for emotional experience. The order in which these human abilities mature must be taken into account. No emotions or attitudes should be generated that would hinder development of reason. Reason itself may be fostered only at the appropriate time. Disregard of these dynamical principles precludes man from acquiring conscience. Their observance is the key to the education of a "natural man."

Rousseau's educational procedure is based on the assumption that the child's autonomous tendencies are sound. He need not, therefore, be subjected to authority. Until reason has developed he should be controlled only through natural discipline. "Keep the child dependent on things only." [2] Nor should he be encouraged to win the approval of others. "Until the time is ripe for the appearance of reason, that guide of selfishness, the main thing is that the child shall do nothing because you are watching him or listening to him; in a word, nothing because of other people, but only what nature asks of him; then he will never do wrong." [3]

The purpose of discipline through things is threefold. Rousseau desires to prevent formation of any habits or psychological needs, especially of a need for power. This is difficult because the child is active and interested in exploring his surroundings. He seeks the help of others and can so acquire a taste for command. From his "own weakness, the source of his first consciousness of dependence, springs the later idea of rule and tyranny." [4] By keeping the child dependent on things only, Rousseau intends to check the growth of any liking for power.

Natural discipline also teaches the child to be self-reliant, to confine his desires within the scope of his own capacities.

2 *Ibid.*, p. 49.   3 *Ibid.*, pp. 56-57.
4 *Ibid.*, p. 33.

Rousseau's plan of education is designed "to give children more real liberty and less power, to let them do more for themselves and demand less of others; so that by teaching them from the first to confine their wishes within the limits of their powers they will scarcely feel the want of whatever is not in their power." [5]

Thirdly, natural discipline prevents development of resentfulness. Since he does not understand its purpose, the child interprets human discipline as malevolence, and this necessarily arouses hate for people. He feels differently toward the recalcitrance of things, because he does not see it as a thwarting of his desires. "For it is in man's nature to bear patiently with the nature of things, but not with the ill-will of another." [6]

By not exposing the child to human discipline Rousseau expects to avoid formation of an emotional structure that would hinder growth of reason. "The education of the earliest years should be merely negative. It consists, not in teaching virtue or truth, but in preserving the heart from vice and from the spirit of error." [7] Its objective is indirectly to facilitate growth of reason but not to force it.

After the period of negative education Rousseau confronts the most serious of all emotional threats to reason. This is pride. The child's feeling of self-respect may develop into either selfishness or concern for the welfare of himself and others. Control of pridefulness and release of moral potentialities call for more positive action. Its purpose is to foster and intensify social emotions. These not only facilitate development of insight and understanding but also inhibit development of selfish feelings. They are essential, therefore, to conversion of man's feeling of self-respect into respect for others, into conscience.

Rousseau's first reference in *Émile* to the awakening of

[5] *Ibid.*, p. 35. [6] *Ibid.*, p. 55.
[7] *Ibid.*, p. 57.

man's conscience is in a description of a child's angry reaction to ill treatment. "Had I doubted the innate sense of
justice and injustice in man's heart, this one instance would
have convinced me." [8]   This feeling has reference only to
the self and its needs. "The first notion of justice springs
not from what we owe to others, but from what is due to
us." [9]   Once the child's abilities exceed his desires, he begins
to have a productive orientation toward others. No longer
concerned only with satisfaction of his own wants, he experiences desire to respond appropriately to the needs of
others. "While we were weak and feeble, self-preservation
concentrated our attention on ourselves; now that we are
strong and powerful, the desire for a wider sphere carries us
beyond ourselves as far as our eyes can reach." [10]   When the
child also becomes aware that others desire to help him, love
for them is evoked. "The child's first sentiment is self-love,
his second, which is derived from it, is love of those about
him." [11]   But love for others gives rise to desire for preference in their eyes. "With love and friendship there begin
dissensions, enmity, and hatred. I behold deference to other
people's opinions enthroned among all these divers passions,
and foolish mortals, enslaved by her power, base their very
existence merely on what other people think." [12]   Expansion
of the child's self brings not only love but also pride, and
with it danger that his attitudes will be shaped by opinion.
If this is permitted to occur, then he will be deprived of his
conscience.

Pride and its accompanying emotions cannot be eliminated
from human nature. This attitude and the emotions to
which it disposes man are necessary aspects of his social experience. But they may be counteracted and neutralized by
deliberate cultivation of social emotions. Sympathy is the

8 *Ibid.*, p. 33.   9 *Ibid.*, p. 61.
10 *Ibid.*, p. 130.   11 *Ibid.*, p. 174.
12 *Ibid.*, p. 176.

"first relative sentiment which touches the human heart according to the order of nature." [13] Once this emotion has appeared, its further development will prevent perversion of self-love into selfishness. "We should arouse in him kindness, goodness, pity, and beneficence, all the gentle and attractive passions which are naturally pleasing to man; those passions prevent the growth of envy, covetousness, hatred, all the repulsive and cruel passions." [14] Thus selfishness may be made to occupy a subordinate place in man's emotional organization. "Only through passion can we gain the mastery over passions; their tyranny must be controlled through their legitimate power, and nature herself must furnish us with the means to control her." [15] Pride is controlled by being placed in a context of social emotions which appear spontaneously but are deliberately intensified.

Along with these transformations of emotional structure there has gone development of the child's intellectual powers. "He has been trained from the outset to be as self-reliant as possible." [16] In this connection Rousseau emphasizes learning for one's self. "Imitation has its roots in our desire to escape from ourselves." [17] Émile must not imitate, for this would render him susceptible to influence of opinion. Nor can there be any reliance on authority of an intellectual kind. This would destroy capacity for independent judgment. "If ever you substitute authority for reason he will cease to reason." [18] "Compelled to learn for himself, he uses his own reason not that of others, for there must be no submission to authority if you would have no submission to convention." [19] Rousseau wishes his student to understand men's behavior and relations. "Our sensations are merely passive, our notions or ideas spring from an active principle which judges." [20] Reason is an "active principle." There

---

[13] *Ibid.*, p. 184.
[15] *Ibid.*, p. 292.
[17] *Ibid.*, p. 68.
[19] *Ibid.*, p. 169.

[14] *Ibid.*
[16] *Ibid.*, p. 83.
[18] *Ibid.*, p. 131.
[20] *Ibid.*, p. 72.

can be no place, therefore, in Rousseau's educational pro-
gram for indoctrination or merely passive absorption of
materials. Man must exercise his own capacity to reason if
he would understand his nature and the significance of his
social relations.

At this stage of his development the child is free from
resentfulness, his social emotions and reason are developing,
and *amour propre* has made its appearance. The question
now is whether he will become a selfish or conscientious being. Rousseau attempts permanently to arrest growth of
egoistic tendencies by showing Émile what he owes to the
benevolence of his fellow man. Recognition of this debt
evokes Émile's feeling of gratitude. "Your pupil, as he begins
to understand the value of your care for him, will be grateful
for it." [21] Appearance of gratitude, accompanied by friendly
affection, marks the emergence of conscience as a full-fledged
sense of justice. "Justice and kindness are no mere abstract
terms, no mere moral conceptions framed by the understanding, but true affections of the heart enlightened by
reason, the natural outcome of our primitive affections." [22]
A sense of justice arises lawfully in the person whose social
emotions and reason have been developed. This attitude is
the product of education in accordance with human dynamics.

Full realization of man's moral potentialities requires two
further steps. By a process of association pride must be displaced from the individual's self and onto humanity. "Extend self-love to others and it is transformed into virtue." [23]
And the scope of compassion must likewise be enlarged.
"To prevent pity degenerating into weakness we must
generalize it and extend it to mankind." [24] Émile learns to
identify himself with the human race. Here Rousseau relies
not on the principle of transformation, which accounts for

[21] *Ibid.*, p. 196.   [22] *Ibid.*
[23] *Ibid.*, p. 215.   [24] *Ibid.*

emergence of man's conscience, but rather on the principle of association, which accounts for man's susceptibility to influence by the opinions of others. This susceptibility is used to reinforce the dictates of reason and conscience.

Thus man in society need not have his attitudes and values determined by opinion. He need not be governed by pridefulness. *Amour propre* is merely one possible, and therefore a contingent, expression of man's social nature. Vanity appears in man before his other capacities have been perfected. When man's reason has developed and through it he grasps the nature of his relationship to his fellows, he necessarily acquires a just attitude toward them. Neither social emotions nor conscience eradicate pride. They do subordinate and control egoistic emotions. In an ideal environment his intellectual development does not make man an antisocial creature who desires to surpass and dominate his fellows. Rather it calls forth his potentiality for justice.

Rousseau views human development as governed by the principle that emotional and intellectual processes are interdependent. Reason develops only in the presence of certain emotional attitudes: independence and freedom from resentfulness. Moral attitudes and emotions have a cognitive basis. They depend on man's understanding of his own needs and on the way he sees his dependence on others. The perfected form of man's intellectual capacity, reason, brings with it of necessity the perfected form of his emotional capacity, conscience. Hence in their perfect forms emotional and intellectual processes do not conflict but rather cooperate in showing man the values and obligations appropriate to his nature. This is to affirm that man is a rational being in the sense that his capacities mesh with each other in moral and value judgments. His sensitivity to his fellows need not stultify reason or obliterate conscience. Given their development, it may conform with and support them.

Conscience, according to Rousseau, is the authentic expression of innate human tendencies, the necessary and specific outcome of the development of man's capacities for self-respect and reason. It is not the product of conditioning or indoctrination, not a "creature of prejudice." For "conscience persists in following the order of nature in spite of all the laws of man." [25] Society does not create conscience in man, rather it calls forth this structure of attitudes. This is not to say, of course, that conscience is a structure of intrinsic attitudes. It would not exist in the absence of beliefs and insights provided by reason.[26]

Together, reason and conscience dictate just behavior, and justice is the value which satisfies man's nature. "Be just and you will be happy." [27] Man is fundamentally moral and social in that when his moral potentialities are fully developed he feels obliged to treat his fellows equally with himself. Presence of this attitude does not, however, guarantee just behavior.

Rousseau draws a sharp distinction between moral judgment and action. Examination of conscience is essential to reliable moral deliberation but insufficient for moral action. "I perceive what is right, I love it, and I do what is wrong." [28] An almost insurmountable element of egoism remains in man. Though he is moved to act on his moral judgments, when these conflict with his personal good, the latter motive is likely to determine behavior. Rousseau refers to " the great moral lesson, perhaps the only one of any practical value, to avoid those situations of life which bring our duties into conflict with our interests." [29] He says, "It is certain that, in such situations, however sincere our love of virtue, we must, sooner or later, inevitably grow weak without per-

25 *Ibid.*, p. 229.
26 Cf. François Bouchardy, "Une Définition de la conscience par J.-J. Rousseau," *Annales de la Société Jean-Jacques Rousseau*, XXXII (1950-52), 167-75.
27 Rousseau, *Émile*, p. 245.   28 *Ibid.*, p. 241.
29 Rousseau, *Confessions*, trans. John Grant, I, 48.

ceiving it, and become unjust and wicked in act, without having ceased to be just and good in our hearts."[30] Here Rousseau verges on psychological hedonism. He does not say that man can never act except for his personal good. But man is liable to bias. He can know his duty, desire to do it, and yet be diverted from its performance by a persistent tendency toward rationalization. Man must, therefore, use his reason to avoid situations in which duty and interest diverge.

Rousseau's reflections on man's personal bias make apparent the extent to which he thinks egoism may be excluded from behavior. In his first and second Discourses, vanity is seen as governing man's behavior, his motives and judgments. He loses contact with his inner sources of direction and seeks satisfaction in the disappointments of others. With release of moral potentialities selfishness is reduced from the status of a total orientation to that of an unconscious bias, one which makes man prone to rationalization but against which he may be on his guard. Given full development of his capacities, man can overcome pride and engage in reliable moral deliberation. The bias that remains in his nature impairs but does not vitiate his capacity for moral actions. Thus moral independence is not beyond the reach of man in society. It depends on his education and maturation in accordance with the autonomous tendencies of his nature.

30 *Ibid.*

3

MORAL
IDEALS

Rousseau's moral ideals are based on his conception of human nature and dynamics. Man is endowed with definite capacities which have a lawful pattern of development. He begins life an egocentric creature concerned only with his own welfare. If his autonomous tendencies are respected, his destiny is to become a moral being guided by reason and conscience. Both the good for man and his fullest satisfaction lie in the exercise of his moral abilities. "Has he not given me conscience that I may love the right, reason that I may perceive it, and freedom that I may choose it?" [1] There is no divergence between ideals for conduct and for character. The ideal man is morally responsible. He performs the obligations prescribed by his moral judgment. "Speak the truth and do the right; the one thing that really matters is to do one's duty in this world." [2]

What Rousseau thinks a person ought to be is difficult to determine because of the way in which he presents his psychological and moral theories. He distinguishes between man in a natural environment and man in society. "Natural man" overlaps these concepts since he uses it to refer to autonomous tendencies or "nature" in man. Some interpretations focus on properties ascribed to man before alteration by social experience, others on man as Rousseau thinks he ought to be in society. In consequence, Rousseau appears

---

[1] Rousseau, *Émile*, p. 257.   [2] *Ibid.*, p. 278.

to embrace different and incompatible ideals. Some see him as a radical individualist, an enemy of reason and discipline. Others see him as an exponent of social discipline so severe as to threaten individuality. Still others argue that he is both, either unaware of his ambiguity or unable to resolve it.

Rousseau does have a coherent ideal for man. But its coherence depends on the idea that human growth, although it may be thwarted, is inherently directed and involves fundamental changes in purpose and orientation. In particular, moral attitudes and values depend on how, and the extent to which, man has developed. It is neglect of this idea that makes Rousseau's moral ideals seem ambiguous. Rousseau does not always remain true to his ideals because he comes to doubt whether moral autonomy and responsibility are consistent with the requirements of political life. In his political writings he sometimes urges men to settle for second best, more easily attainable ideals. But this Rousseau cannot do without violation of man's moral potentialities and disregard for his moral destiny. Not ambiguity of ideals but doubt of their attainability is the source of Rousseau's vacillations.

Rousseau is said to disparage use of reason. According to Irving Babbitt, he is the fountainhead of "romanticism" and wants man to rely on urges of his "ordinary self" for moral guidance.[3] John Herman Randall, Jr., says that for Rousseau "the natural man is not the rational thinker, judging everything by its usefulness to himself and his fellows, but rather the man of passion and feeling."[4] John Bowle says, "Rousseau admires the average man: he wants to level out the actual inequalities of men by stressing moral intuition

[3] Babbitt, *Rousseau and Romanticism*, p. 128. Babbitt contends that depreciation of reason and exaltation of emotion are central to the doctrine of "romanticism." But compare Jacques Barzun, *Romanticism and the Modern Ego*.

[4] Randall, *The Making of the Modern Mind*, p. 401.

and character, often at the expense of disciplined intelligence." [5] Another political theorist argues that "all restraint upon man's natural impulses Rousseau believes is bad—goodness consists in being liberated from law, from discipline, from authority, from the obligations imposed by God and our fellow man." [6] All these writers appear to underestimate the role Rousseau assigns to reason in human affairs. "When I want to train a natural man, I do not want to make him a savage and to send him back to the woods, but that living in the whirl of social life it is enough that he should not let himself be carried away by the passions and prejudices of men: let him see with his eyes and feel with his heart, let him own no sway but that of reason." [7] Rousseau thinks that reason is an emergent characteristic of man. This does not mean that he depreciates it. Its use is indispensable both to the formation of conscience and to reliable moral decision making. Rousseau does not contrast and oppose sentiment to reason. He attributes both cognitive and conative functions to emotions and attitudes, but these always have a cognitive foundation. [8]

The concepts "state of nature" and "natural man" are Rousseau's analytical tools. In his intellectual climate they were accepted ways of talking about human nature. It is not surprising, therefore, that he uses them to alert his society to values he thinks inappropriate to man. As Alfred Cobban says, "The conception of natural man provides Rousseau with an ideal, a standard by which to measure social and political institutions." [9] Ernst Cassirer points out that Rousseau uses the concept, "state of nature," "as a standard and norm according to which he can show what in

5 Bowle, *Western Political Thought: An Historical Introduction from the Origins to Rousseau*, p. 416.
  6 John H. Hallowell, *Main Currents in Modern Political Thought*, p. 173.
  7 Rousseau, *Émile*, p. 217.
  8 See William Boyd, *The Educational Theory of Jean Jacques Rousseau*, pp. 166-67.
  9 Cobban, *Rousseau and the Modern State*, p. 221.

the present state of society is truth and what illusion, what is morally obligatory law and what is mere convention and caprice." [10] These concepts should not be given a historical meaning. Rousseau does not intend to send men "back" to a "state of nature." He is criticizing their way of life and ideals.

Rousseau is appalled by the impact of urban civilization on man's character and life. Some of his most bitter diatribes are directed against the city. "Men are devoured by our towns." [11] In an urban environment autonomy is blighted and materialism is encouraged. His preference for a rural way of life is based on the independence and peacefulness it sustains. "If there is any safe and lawful way of living without intrigues, without lawsuits, without dependence on others, it is . . . to live by the labor of our hands, by the cultivation of our own land." [12] It is concern for autonomy and justice that makes him critical of his society. As John Stuart Mill says, "The superior worth of simplicity of life, the enervating and demoralizing effect of the trammels and hypocrisies of artificial society, are ideas which have never been entirely absent from cultivated minds since Rousseau wrote." [13]

Looking behind terminology to the essence of Rousseau's critique of civilization, we find little more than what since has become a commonplace of social theory. William Ernest Hocking refers to the operation of a "law of decline" in complex society.[14] Charles Horton Cooley observes that

10 Cassirer, *The Philosophy of the Enlightenment,* trans. Fritz C. A Koelln and James P. Pettegrove, p. 271.

11 Rousseau, *Émile,* p. 26.   12 *Ibid.,* p. 421.

13 John Stuart Mill, *On Liberty,* p. 41.

14 Hocking says that in the advanced society, *"self assertive dispositions increase.* For satisfactions increase, and with them the expectation and demand that *all* wants be satisfied. . . . At the same time, *the natural checks upon self-assertion diminish.* For as the whole grows larger, and the circuits of cause and effect within it harder to trace, it becomes to the average imagination less vividly real, and the ends it pursues increasingly remote from tangible objectives" (*Man and the State,* pp. 303-4).

"every general increase of freedom is accompanied by some degeneracy." [15] And Robert M. MacIver says, "Anomy is a disease of the civilized, not of the simpler peoples." [16] Here is reflected concern, similar to Rousseau's doubt of the desirability of urban life, that as society becomes more complicated men tend to become materialistic and morally irresponsible. In this light Rousseau's appraisal of his civilization appears less sinister than when cast in the form of denigration of reason and progress. He was disturbed by what he considered the complacency of his contemporaries in the face of moral evils. He also had grave doubts about the eighteenth-century idea of progress.[17] But he does not advise men to stop trying to improve themselves and their society through use of reason.

Rousseau's references to a *moi commun* [18] are taken by some to indicate acceptance of an organic view of the relation between individuals and society. MacIver says that such a view has "no proper place for the autonomy, the initiative, the selfhood, the personality, of the individual." [19] It implies that individuals derive their worth from society and ought, therefore, to adopt an attitude of uncritical devotion to it. That society is an "organism" may also be thought to imply existence of a "group mind" which is more enlightened than, and therefore superior to, any individual mind.

Rousseau does think people are both psychologically and morally dependent on their society. Only in and through society can they realize their potentialities. But this does not imply the existence of any entity superordinate to individuals. "He who had a perfect knowledge of the inclina-

15 Cooley, *Human Nature and the Social Order,* p. 403.
16 MacIver, *The Ramparts We Guard,* p. 87.
17 See J. B. Bury, *The Idea of Progress: An Inquiry into Its Origin and Growth,* pp. 177ff.
18 For example, *The Social Contract,* Book i, ch. 6.
19 Robert M. MacIver, *The Web of Government,* p. 408.

tions of each individual might foresee all their combined effects in the body of the nation." [20]   Individuals are transformed by society, but this does not mean that society is anything more than a synthesis of their effects on one another.   Rousseau's conception of the relation between persons and society is comparable to that of a "psychological group" the members of which are in "dynamic interaction" with one another.[21]

It is also true, as John Plamenatz points out, that Rousseau thinks "human societies develop in accordance with laws unknown to their members, whose characters, beliefs and purposes are profoundly altered by that development." [22]   But neither this principle nor that of social dependence implies that individuals are not centers of value or ought not to be sources of initiative and judgment.   Indeed, Rousseau asserts that without moral autonomy the social process is distorted and people acquire inappropriate values and attitudes. Man can realize his potentialities as a moral being only through the exercise of his capacity for self-determination.

Bernard Bosanquet says that "for Rousseau's political theory everything turns on the reality of the 'moral person' which constitutes the State." [23]   If the strain of psychological hedonism in Rousseau's thinking is disregarded, it can be argued that he does envisage a moral ideal that goes beyond satisfaction of the claims of justice.   Ideally man

20 Rousseau, *Émile*, p. 202.
21 David Krech and Richard S. Crutchfield say that the "criteria for establishing whether or not a given set of individuals constitutes a psychological group are mainly two: (1) All the members must exist as a group in the psychological field of each individual, *i.e.*, be perceived and reacted to as a group; (2) the various members must be in dynamic interaction with one another." By "dynamic interaction" they mean that "the behavior of each one affects all the others, these effects rebound on the original member who in turn influences all the others anew, and this complex of effects is taking place simultaneously among all members" (*Theory and Problems of Social Psychology*, pp. 367-68).
22 Plamenatz, *The English Utilitarians*, p. 155.
23 Bosanquet, *The Philosophical Theory of the State*, p. 96.

should think more of his duties and less of his rights, and should deal with his fellows in a spirit of loving kindness. This conception of moral responsibility, however, is quite compatible with selfhood of individuals and does not involve the existence of a "group mind." [24]

Rousseau's thought is said to contain an irreducible duality of ideals. Man may be "natural" and preserve his autonomy only by withdrawing from society. Or he may be "social," which entails submergence in the group. According to Bernard Groethuysen, Rousseau sees "natural" and "social" man as alternative ideals:

Natural man and social man represent two ways of life essentially different. To be natural, man ought to liberate himself from the yoke of public opinion, he ought to detach himself from vanity, he has to know how to live within himself. In the social state, on the contrary, it is public judgment which ought to rule the individual life. . . . Vanity, far from being a defect, constitutes one of the strongest supports of social life; it allies itself with patriotism, it engenders emulation which incites the citizen to distinguish himself in the service of his country. . . . No one ought to isolate himself, shut off his existence, all ought to live the life of the community.[25]

Man must choose. Either he can be "natural" or he can be "social." Choice of one ideal involves rejection of the other.

Rousseau does distinguish between "natural" and "social" man. But the distinction is not quite so sharp as Groethuysen attempts to make out. "Social" man is not entirely different from "natural" man. Creation of the former does involve disregard of the autonomous tendencies and their pattern of development, which is scrupulously adhered to in the education of the latter. "Social" man is a

24 Otto Gierke says, "Even for Rousseau, the social body is in the last analysis only a mechanically constituted Whole, with a life which only resides in the life of its parts" (*Natural Law and the Theory of Society*, trans. Ernest Barker, I, 136).

25 Groethuysen, *Jean-Jacques Rousseau*, p. 117. Author's translation.

creature of associative processes. He is built upon man's susceptibility to influence from his fellows. But some of his characteristics are those of "natural" man. In particular, man in society must retain some measure of autonomy if social processes are not to become maladaptive and destructive of his welfare. Moreover, it is doubtful that Rousseau offers man a choice between competing, equally valid ideals, as Groethuysen suggests. Moral autonomy and responsibility are the higher ideals. But they may be unobtainable for political reasons which force men, in Rousseau's view, to choose between the lower ideal and subjection to tyrannical regimes.

Consider Groethuysen's contention that Rousseau would liberate "natural" man from, and subjugate "social" man to, public opinion. It is true that in his later work Rousseau does envisage making men very responsive to the opinions of and pressure from their group. But we ought not to confuse the two processes by which Rousseau thinks man acquires attitudes and values. When he says man ought to liberate himself from public opinion he means that man ought to rely on his own reason and conscience instead of acquiring his values from others under the influence of vanity. When he says that public opinion ought to govern the individual's behavior he can mean, as we shall show, that because of personal bias, valid moral decisions are likely to be the product of group deliberation. But the validity of the group's decision depends on the integrity of each individual's contribution, on each relying on his own reason and conscience. Thus reliable moral and political deliberation may involve both freedom from public opinion and acceptance of public judgment. Indeed, the one is a condition essential to the other. What is common, in this case, to both "natural" and "social" man is moral autonomy. There is here no duality of ideals. Social men cannot both submit completely to public opinion and arrive at valid moral decisions. Respect for public opinion need not mean mutual reflection of attitudes and values under the influence of vanity.

The contention that "natural" man is not prideful, but that "social" man ought to be, is more serious but still does not prove that Rousseau has no coherent, unique ideal for man. The question it raises is whether Rousseau's view of the requirements of moral action is consistent with his view of the requirements of moral deliberation in terms of his own theory of human nature and dynamics. In society man is bound to experience pride, but this emotion need not be so intense as to govern his judgments and behavior. Pride may be controlled by placing it in a web of social emotions and by making its focus the group. It does impair man's moral judgment, limit the scope of moral deliberation, and make him prone to rationalization. But invalid judgments may be avoided by group deliberation and just action ensured by adherence to law. Despite the defect of pride, then, man can achieve moral goodness and responsibility. If, however, right action in the political realm can be obtained from man only by intensifying pride and converting it into patriotism, then doubt arises as to whether this is consistent with reliable moral deliberation so far as this depends on the exercise of reason and the consultation of conscience. For, according to Rousseau's theory of human nature and dynamics, pridefulness makes these impossible. In this case, as Groethuysen contends, "social" man is indeed a creature different from "natural" man. He is patriotic and responsive to the opinion of his group rather than rational and conscientious. His moral potentialities have been violated. This is to say that he is something less than the human ideal.

Rousseau holds out to man the twin ideals of moral autonomy and responsibility. If his notion of a "return to nature" is understood as a demand for reassertion of individuality, and if his concept of a *moi commun* is understood to refer to the reality of man's moral potentialities, then there is no inconsistency or duality in his conception of the good for man. Moral independence is the basis of moral goodness and responsibility. Rousseau's ideal man is governed by reason and conscience, is independent, yet alert to the danger of personal bias. Rousseau does not think, as Leo Strauss suggests, that "man is by nature almost infinitely malleable." [26] Man is not plastic with respect to values. The dynamics of his nature do make possible different lines of development for him. He is plastic with respect to motives in that he may act either as his conscience dictates or to gain the approval of his group. But there is only one line of development that is fully in accord with man's nature, the one that releases his moral self. Only justice and benevolence can fully satisfy this self.

[26] Strauss, *Natural Right and History*, p. 271.

Part Two

POLITICAL THEORY

Il faut étudier la société par les hommes, et les hommes par la société: ceux qui voudront traiter séparément la politique et la morale n'entendront jamais rien à aucune des deux.

ÉMILE, BOOK IV

4

INSTITUTIONAL REQUIREMENTS OF HUMAN NATURE

Rousseau's political theory attempts to solve the problem of how man may achieve moral goodness. How can men endowed with the potentialities of reason and conscience, yet tending always to seek their personal goods, associate with one another, legislate for their common welfare, and govern themselves consistently with this ideal? Vanity blurs their vision of the morally obligatory, self-interest diverts them from it, yet goodness demands that they arrive at valid decisions, translate them into law, and despite the pressure of their biases maintain the integrity of that law.

Rousseau discards the traditional Christian view that only with the help of God's grace can man become morally good. He holds that man's endowment is sufficient to this challenge, to meet it his responsibility alone. Man is biased but not depraved; his judgments and actions are not hopelessly warped by original sin. Not through grace but through law does man overcome and transcend his hedonistic tendencies. Society is his sacred right, for virtue cannot be a personal achievement. Either men attain to goodness together or not at all.

Rousseau cannot accept either the Platonic view that pridefulness may be eradicated from some few men whose duty it is to govern the rest according to their intuition of goodness. This presumes that moral bias is not integral to man in society. Platonism also involves a denial of moral freedom, which Rousseau holds essential to moral insight. Not in eradication but in evasion of vanity does he see man attaining to goodness. Man can have confidence in moral and political decisions only by deliberately restricting their scope. His actions may be saved from the corrupting influence of self-interest by law that is of general applicability.

In two respects Rousseau's political theory is Aristotelian. He thinks group deliberation more likely to be right than any individual's judgment. Under certain conditions, individuals' biases are mutually correcting, not reinforcing. Also, he tries to use their pridefulness to induce men to perform politically necessary functions. Here doubt arises whether this use of pride, especially when its deliberate intensification is involved, can be compatible with either moral freedom or reliable moral deliberation. This is to ask whether Rousseau's political theory is consistent with his psychological theory and moral ideals. Will the institutions he prescribes for man enable him to realize the values appropriate to his nature?

Given his view of human nature and ideals, Rousseau must design a society in which man's moral potentialities are released and his egoistic biases neutralized. This society is based on three main principles. Its institutions should develop and sustain moral independence and freedom. This is essential if man's attitudes and values are to be functions of insight and not of opinion. Secondly, because of their tendency toward rationalization, men's interests ought not to be placed in opposition to their obligations. And thirdly, pridefulness should facilitate, not hinder, men's use of reason and reliance on conscience. These principles determine the institutional requirements of human nature. Institutions inconsistent with them necessarily involve violations of man's moral potentialities.

The purpose of this Part is to identify Rousseau's applications of, and deviations from, these principles in his political theory. This chapter deals with their implications for the way in which men may legitimately associate with one another. In the following chapter, their application in techniques of legislation and government is analyzed. Chapter Six examines the reasons why, and the methods by which, Rousseau attempts to intensify man's social sentiment. Some of these methods are shown to be incompatible with realization of his moral ideals. This Part concludes with an appraisal of the view that Rousseau's political theory is essentially totalitarian.

According to Rousseau, the fundamental problem of political organization is "to find a form of association which will defend and protect with the whole common force the person and goods of each associate, and in which each, while uniting himself with all, may still obey himself alone, and remain as free as before." [1] Application of two of his principles provides Rousseau with the solution.

If men are to associate without conflict between duty and interest, Rousseau holds they must adopt a form of association in which they are both mutually and totally dependent on one another. He prescribes "the total alienation of each associate, together with all his rights, to the whole community; for, in the first place, as each gives himself absolutely, the conditions are the same for all; and, this being so, no one has any interest in making them burdensome to others." [2] Rousseau neutralizes man's egoistic tendencies by forcing him to identify his interests with those of his fellows.

Preservation of man's independence is accomplished by placing him under the authority of the "general will." *"Each of us puts his person and all his power in common under the supreme direction of the general will, and, in our corporate capacity, we receive each member as an indivisible*

[1] Rousseau, *The Social Contract*, Book I, ch. 6.
[2] *Ibid.*

part of the whole." [3]   Acceptance of the authority of the "general will" excludes submission to any personal authority. But it is to man's selfish interest to establish a personal authority and acquire power over his fellows. It is inevitable that some will attempt this. Therefore, the social contract

tacitly includes the undertaking, which alone can give force to the rest, that whoever refuses to obey the general will shall be compelled to do so by the whole body. This means nothing less than that he will be forced to be free; for this is the condition which, by giving each citizen to his country, secures him against all personal dependence. In this lies the key to the working of the political machine; this alone legitimizes civil undertakings, which, without it, would be absurd, tyrannical, and liable to the most frightful abuses.[4]

All must agree not only to obey the general will but also to enforce it. For unless the general will is enforced all lose their independence. The one who acquires power necessarily becomes dependent on the others since he must rule them through prejudice and opinion, without regard for the dictates of reason and conscience. Submission to him destroys the moral freedom of the others. In Rousseau's society the moral freedom of each depends on the moral freedom of all.

Once men have associated in this manner, their moral potentialities are released.

The passage from the state of nature to the civil state produces a very remarkable change in man, by substituting justice for instinct in his conduct, and giving his actions the morality they had formerly lacked. Then only, when the voice of duty takes the place of physical impulses and right of appetite, does man, who so far had considered only himself, find that he is forced to act on different principles, and to consult his reason before listening to his inclinations.[5]

3 *Ibid.*   4 *Ibid.*, Book i, ch. 7.
5 *Ibid.*, Book i, ch. 8.

Above all man acquires "moral liberty, which alone makes him truly master of himself; for the mere impulse of appetite is slavery, while obedience to a law which we prescribe to ourselves is liberty." [6]

These changes in man are not, of course, to be thought of as taking place instantaneously with the making of the contract. Rousseau is speaking rather of what will happen to a person in a properly organized society. The individual is no longer a purely self-interested creature who lacks a sense of justice. His relation to his fellows forces him to use his reason, and since he is under the authority or power of no person, this evokes his conscience. He can act as his reason and conscience dictate since his actions are governed by law. This law is the expression of his own reason and conscience. Hence man is morally free as well as morally responsible.

These passages contain the essence of Rousseau's view of the kind of political association appropriate to the dynamics of human nature. It is the organizational counterpart of his system of education. Its essential feature is that no person has authority over the others. Man's own egoism precludes this. But more importantly, the existence of personal authority would deprive men of their right to moral development and freedom. Mutual dependence on law is the only morally legitimate basis of association. Through dependence on law men are enabled to associate without morally stultifying personal dependence. Through law each is enabled to defeat his hedonistic tendencies. Law both releases and fulfills man's moral potentialities.

Does Rousseau's conception of the proper form of political association involve—whether or not he intends it—man's submission to his group? Does he substitute for personal dependence a group dependence which is equally destructive of moral autonomy and responsibility?

6 *Ibid.*

The social contract does involve total alienation of the rights which man is presumed to have in the "state of nature." In effect, Rousseau repudiates the notion of natural rights as rights which man may carry over from the "state of nature" to society. But this need not imply man's subordination to society. Rousseau's whole argument rests on the assumption that man has a right to the development of his moral potentialities, and consequently a right to the form of social and political organization which makes that development possible. His right to self-government is, therefore, absolute. "To renounce liberty is to renounce being a man, to surrender the rights of humanity and even its duties. For him who renounces everything no indemnity is possible. Such a renunciation is incompatible with man's nature; to remove all liberty from his will is to remove all morality from his acts." [7] As man cannot submit to a personal authority without depriving himself of the possibility of moral action, neither can he submit to society. He cannot relinquish autonomy without denying his nature as a moral being.

Even granted that Rousseau thinks moral freedom integral to man's nature, does he not indicate that he fails to understand its meaning by his assertion that a person can be "forced to be free"? If freedom is defined as absence of restraint alone, then Rousseau's contention does not make sense. But he does not define freedom in this way. Freedom to Rousseau means self-determination in the sense of inner determination, of use of, and reliance upon, one's own capacity for moral judgment and action. It does not mean only absence of personal dependence, that is, freedom in a political sense. What, then, does he mean to say by the statement that a person can be forced to be free? Bernard Bosanquet says that Rousseau intends to distinguish between the freedom of the "physical individual" and that of the "social person." "If the social person is taken as the reality,

7 *Ibid.*, Book I, ch. 4.

it follows, as Rousseau points out, that force against the physical individual may become a condition of freedom." [8] If we substitute for Bosanquet's expression "the physical individual" the notion of man's ineradicable egoistic tendencies, then his statement comes very close to expressing Rousseau's meaning. Man desires power. But power destroys the moral freedom of all parties to the relationship. "One thinks himself the master of others, and still remains a greater slave than they." [9] From Rousseau's standpoint, to prevent a person from obtaining power is to force that person to be free. Lack of power over others is a condition of his freedom, of the development of his reason and conscience, of his life in a society based on law.

Rousseau's use of the word "free" in this way may appear illiberal to many and especially to those who would maintain that freedom means only absence of restraint. But if we look to what Rousseau intends to say and disregard his peculiar use of the word "free," it is seen that he neither intends nor achieves subordination of the individual to society. His concern is to establish a society based on morally obligatory law, which in his view is the prerequisite to individual moral freedom. "It is not true that he gains nothing from the laws; they give him courage to be just, even in the midst of the wicked. It is not true that they have failed to make him free; they have taught him to rule himself." [10] Given Rousseau's theory of human nature, it is logical to presume that individuals will seek to evade or subvert the general will, and that this would destroy the autonomy of all. For social men the alternatives are mutual dependence on law or personal dependence and loss of moral integrity.

It is illuminating to consider Rousseau's conception of the right form of political and social organization in the light of

8 Bosanquet, *The Philosophical Theory of the State*, p. 90.
9 Rousseau, *The Social Contract*, Book I, ch. 1.
10 Rousseau, *Émile*, p. 437.

the passage in *Émile* in which he analyzes the forms of human dependence.

There are two kinds of dependence: dependence on things, which is the work of nature; and dependence on men, which is the work of society. Dependence on things, being non-moral, does no injury to liberty and begets no vices; dependence on men, being out of order, gives rise to every kind of vice, and through this master and slave become mutually depraved. If there is any cure for this social evil, it is to be found in the substitution of law for the individual; in arming the general will with a real strength beyond the power of any individual will. If the laws of nations, like the laws of nature, could never be broken by any human power, dependence on men would become dependence on things; all the advantages of a state of nature would be combined with all the advantages of social life in the commonwealth. The liberty which preserves a man from vice would be united with the morality which raises him to virtue.[11]

Dependence on nature is compatible with moral freedom, dependence on individual men is not. In society law is the substitute for nature. It enables men to relate to one another without experiencing the corrupting influence of power. It preserves men from vanity and so makes possible moral deliberation. It curbs their self-interest and so makes possible moral action. Thus law is more than just a substitute for nature. Outside society there can be neither moral freedom nor goodness, simply absence of moral evil. Law enables men not only to live together in freedom but also to achieve goodness.

With respect to the significance of law, *The Social Contract* may be regarded as the supplement to *Émile*. What Rousseau does is to attempt to transfer the individual from dependence on nature to dependence on law. In this way he hopes to sustain the moral autonomy which he regards as the product of his educational methods. Each citizen should

11 *Ibid.*, p. 49.

be "perfectly independent of all the rest, and at the same time very dependent on the city." [12] His aim is to combine moral independence with political dependence, not on any one person but on the group. Mutual dependence on and through law is both the successor to dependence on nature and the only alternative to personal dependence.

If this were all there is to Rousseau's political theory, we should be justified in saying that he has merely taken men out of a situation in which they are disciplined by "things" and placed them in a situation where they discipline each other. True, men agree to obey the general will, which is the legal expression of their reason and conscience. But they also agree to enforce it, and, as Rousseau points out, this is the crucial clause of the contract. So long as each seeks to evade the general will, the contract would provide hardly more than a system of mutual coercion. Self-determination would remain an illusion. Although the law may be an expression of the reason and conscience of each, his motive for obedience is its sanction, not the discharge of his duty to his fellows. But the contract should be thought of as providing an institutional environment which accords with the requirements of man's nature, which fosters development of his moral potentialities. Life in society under guidance of the general will not only neutralizes man's egoistic tendencies and forces him to consider his duties. It also gives rise to social sentiment and spirit as he becomes accustomed to, and grows to like, social life. Although he has no instinct of sociability, man becomes interested in, and emotionally involved with, his group. His attitude toward the law changes from that of reluctant obedience to that of positive acceptance. The contract establishes the conditions essential to this psychological development. Its completion is the work of the law and the political machine through which it is made.

[12] Rousseau, *The Social Contract*, Book II, ch. 12.

Chapter

5

THE
POLITICAL
MACHINE

WITH THE BEGINNING of social life there arises in man a conflict between two motives rooted in his contradictory nature. He experiences both the desire to be just and the desire to pursue his personal good without regard for the welfare of others. Man's desire for justice Rousseau calls his general will, his desire for preference his particular will. In the course of social development particular will is subordinated to general will, provided that man governs himself through appropriate political institutions. The aim of this chapter is to reveal the nature of these institutions. But first we must see just how Rousseau envisages the conflicting motives that arise in man in society.

That man has a general will is the necessary consequence of his nature and the form of association created by the contract. Man desires his own welfare. In so far as this is bound up with the welfare of all, he must desire the common welfare also. According to Rousseau, this desire for the common welfare cannot be extinguished so long as men's interests are interdependent. Even though an individual has interests in conflict with the common interest, he must still desire and will the latter. "Apart from this particular good, he wills the general good in his own interest, as strongly as any one else." [1] In this sense the general will is indestructible, that is to say, man in so far as he is rational recognizes

1 Rousseau, *The Social Contract,* Book IV, ch. 1.

that what is to the general interest is also to his personal
interest.   But rational self-interest is not all that Rousseau
means by his concept of a general will.   It is the expression
not only of man's reason but also of his conscience, of his
desire for justice and goodness.   He knows that the general
will is the motive upon which he ought to act.   This is his
duty, not merely a calculation of expediency.   But this desire for justice is opposed by man's desire for his personal
good.   The problem that confronts Rousseau is how this
conflict of motives may be resolved.   Otherwise man would
remain in a condition of perpetual tension, torn between
duty and desire, driven one way by his conscience and
another by his self-interest.

Rousseau's solution may be approached through analysis
of his concept of the political machine.   Once a general will
has arisen in man and before it has become his governing
motive, this desire for justice must be translated into law.
This is the function of the political machine.   It is designed
to convert general will into morally obligatory law.   It makes
the general will operative.   Given the existence of valid law,
there arises in man a social sentiment, the effect of which is
that he no longer feels the law a restraint but rather the expression of his moral purpose.   It is essential to keep in mind
that Rousseau thinks man's socialization is a gradual process.
"For a young people to be able to relish sound principles of
political theory and follow the fundamental rules of state-
craft, the effect would have to become the cause; the social
spirit, which should be created by these institutions, would
have to preside over their very foundation; and men would
have to be before law what they should become by means of
law." [2]   Man's moral potentialities are fully realized only
when he has acquired "social spirit."   This is the sentiment,
which enables him to subordinate his selfish desires to his
will for justice.

The political machine is based on the mutual dependence

[2] *Ibid.*, Book II, ch. 7.

of men established by the contract. Rousseau refers to absence of personal dependence as "the key to the working of
the political machine." [3] Given this condition, the machine
may be said to consist of three institutions. First, individuals
exercise their own judgment as to what justice and the
general welfare require. Second, legislation is of general
applicability. And third, approximate economic equality
exists. We shall examine each of these institutions in turn
and show how it is implied by Rousseau's theory of human
nature.

Independence of judgment is required to ascertain what
justice requires because of the necessity for mutual correction
of personal bias. Individuals desire to legislate for the
general welfare, but the judgment of each as to what it requires may well be incorrect. "The general will is always
right and tends to the public advantage; but it does not
follow that the deliberations of the people are always equally
correct. Our will is always for our own good, but we do not
always see what that is; the people is never corrupted, but it
is often deceived, and on such occasions only does it seem to
will what is bad." [4] To the extent that men's interests are
identical, they can be confident of arriving at a sound decision. Where interests diverge, personal bias begins to
operate. Public deliberation can reach a just decision because men's desires for their personal goods tend to offset
each other in a mechanical fashion. For this to happen they
must all desire and seek the course of action that is in the
general welfare. Otherwise their biases may seem to coincide
to dictate a course of action which is not really for the
general welfare. In this case, the general will is not expressed but rather the "will of all." "There is often a great
deal of difference between the will of all and the general
will; the latter considers only the common interest, while
the former takes private interest into account, and is no

3 *Ibid.*, Book i, ch. 7.   4 *Ibid.*, Book ii, ch. 3.

more than a sum of particular wills: but take away from these same wills the pluses and minuses that cancel one another, and the general will remains as the sum of the differences." [5] Expression of the general will cannot be a purely mechanical process in which conflicting personal goods merely offset and cancel each other. This they do, but only if each of the participants is motivated by desire for the general welfare and actively seeks to discover the course of action that promotes it. "When in the popular assembly a law is proposed, what the people is asked is not exactly whether it approves or rejects the proposal, but whether it is in conformity with the general will, which is their will." [6] Each must attempt to determine the course of action that will produce the greatest amount of happiness that is consistent with justice for the community.

Rousseau assumes that the larger the number of biases the smaller and milder each is likely to be and, therefore, the more easily each can be corrected. It is essential, "if the general will is to be able to express itself, that there should be no partial society within the State, and that each citizen should think only his own thoughts." [7] Rousseau fears that the presence of "partial societies" reduces the number and increases the magnitude of biases, which leads to distortion of the group's judgment. Hence, he says, "If there are partial societies, it is best to have as many as possible and to prevent them from being unequal." [8] No group of persons should be able to impose its will upon the rest.

Given adequate information and lacking opportunity for composition of differences by logrolling, the people can engage in reliable moral deliberation and so express their general will. Its expression is essentially a process of "dynamic interaction" in which individuals do not merely reflect one another's judgments but actively strive to correct

[5] *Ibid.*
[7] *Ibid.*, Book II, ch. 3.
[6] *Ibid.*, Book IV, ch. 2.
[8] *Ibid.*

them. Even though their judgments are influenced by their personal goods and their group attachments, they can still reach a valid decision if each individual makes an independent estimate of what the law should be.

The distinctive thing about the general will is that its expression requires both individual integrity and group effort. It can be "enlightened," [9] the limitations of individuals' judgments can be transcended, only through group deliberation. But successful deliberation demands that each participant maintain independence of judgment. If he does not, there is no guarantee that all biases will be revealed and eliminated. It is mutual revelation of bias that makes it possible for the group to reach a valid decision. If each permits the other to hold a view in which personal good predominates, the result of discussion will be an expression of the "will of all." In this case, it is possible for the group to reach an agreement that is unanimous and yet mistaken. The result of deliberation may be consensus, but if this is to be valid, each participant must strive to define the dictates of his own reason and conscience.

The second institutional component of Rousseau's political machine is that legislation deal only with matters of common concern. This appears to mean both that the subject of legislation must be restricted to matters which are seen by all to relate to the general welfare, to those aspects of welfare which are common to all; and that legislation must, if not actually at least potentially, apply to all, to each individual. The purpose of this requirement is to guard the individual against the selfish tendencies present in all. "If it is not impossible for a particular will to agree on some point with the general will, it is at least impossible for the agreement to be lasting and constant; for the particular will tends, by its very nature, to partiality, while the general will tends to equality." [10] As we have seen, Rousseau concludes

9 *Ibid.*   10 *Ibid.*, Book II, ch. 1.

from the presence of a selfish tendency in man that he must not be placed in a situation where his personal good conflicts with his obligation to others. If legislative judgment is to be valid, its scope must be restricted to matters of common interest. "It is solely on the basis of this common interest that every society should be governed." [11]

Each individual may be presumed to know what is good for himself and to demand justice for himself. By placing him in a position where this demand necessarily includes justice for all, Rousseau hopes to enable the group to reach a just decision. The general will "loses its natural rectitude when it is directed to some particular and determinate object, because in such a case we are judging of something foreign to us, and have no true principle of equity to guide us." [12] Man's own welfare must be at stake; otherwise personal bias may lead him to impose on others laws which he would not be willing to accept for himself. "What makes the will general is less the number of voters than the common interest uniting them; for, under this system, each necessarily submits to the conditions he imposes on others: and this admirable agreement between interest and justice gives to the common deliberations an equitable character which at once vanishes when any particular question is discussed, in the absence of a common interest to unite and identify the ruling of the judge with that of the party." [13] General applicability of legislation makes it to the interest of each that the legislation be just, for it will apply to him. Otherwise he would be tempted to sacrifice the welfare of others to his own. By restricting legislation to matters of common concern, Rousseau forces each to limit his pursuit of personal good out of regard for the personal goods of others. Thus duty and desire, justice and interest, are made to coincide.

11 *Ibid.*
13 *Ibid.*

12 *Ibid.*, Book II, ch. 4.

Together, independence of individual judgment and legislative generality ensure that laws will be both in the public interest and consistent with the requirements of justice. Such laws meet the demands of the individual's moral consciousness and, therefore, are obligatory upon him. He may desire to do more for his fellows and feel that he has greater obligations to them than those defined by the law. But, given his bias for personal good, reliable moral deliberation is possible only through the group in accordance with the institutions of the political machine. The general will as translated into law prescribes the limits within which the individual may be certain of achieving moral goodness. Outside the framework of the law lies a realm of moral darkness and doubt.

The third institutional component of the political machine is substantial economic equality. Here Rousseau's concern is with making personal independence effective.

If we ask in what precisely consists the greatest good of all, which should be the end of every system of legislation, we shall find it reduce itself to two main objects, liberty and equality—liberty, because all particular dependence means so much force taken from the body of the State, and equality, because liberty cannot exist without it.[14]

He means by equality "not that the degrees of power and riches are to be absolutely identical for everybody; but that power shall never be great enough for violence, and shall always be exercised by virtue of rank and law; and that, in respect of riches, no citizen shall ever be wealthy enough to buy another, and none poor enough to be forced to sell himself."[15] This is not a demand for absolute equality, but for a degree sufficient to prevent anyone from acquiring power and influence over others. Any form of personal dependence, whether it be political, economic, or social, Rousseau regards as a threat to a person's moral integrity. If the

[14] *Ibid.*, Book II, ch. 11.   [15] *Ibid.*

general will is to be expressed, all must be free to state their own opinions as to what justice and the public interest require.

Through the institutions of the political machine, men create for themselves an environment of just law, and by doing so alter their attitudes. They acquire a new orientation toward their society and its laws. Their attitude toward justice and the general welfare becomes more positive. Expression of the general will becomes less of a mechanical process in which opposing interests cancel each other and more of an active search for justice and goodness. Rousseau refers to law,

which is not graven on tablets of marble or brass, but on the hearts of the citizens. This forms the real constitution of the State, takes on every day new powers, when other laws decay or die out, restores them or takes their place, keeps a people in the ways in which it was meant to go, and insensibly replaces authority by the force of habit. I am speaking of morality, of custom, above all of public opinion; a power unknown to political thinkers, on which none the less success in everything else depends.[16]

Life in society under authority of the general will socializes and moralizes men. They become habituated to social life and the law. Conformity to the general will becomes less the product of respect for authority and more a matter of inclination. Their attitude toward the law changes. They regard it less as a constraint and more as the expression of their moral purpose.

Rousseau calls these developments in man "the real constitution of the State." General will is ascendant over man's particular will. Bias remains, but purpose has changed. Man is no longer egocentric, concentrated upon his own welfare. His purposes include the welfare of his fellows. It is no longer accurate to speak of him as being "forced"

16 *Ibid.*, Book II, ch. 12.

"to consult his reason before listening to his inclinations." [17]
He is becoming "truly master of himself." [18]

If we summarize the results of our analysis of Rousseau's
political machine, it is apparent that it is designed to translate man's desire for justice into law and thereby to
strengthen his moral purpose. Through its institutions men
are enabled to produce a body of just law, life under which
develops and sustains in them a social attitude. This social
spirit should be distinguished from man's sense of justice.
It is more a feeling of interest and concern than of obligation. It is the outcome of man's capacity for sympathetic
response to the needs of his fellows and his ability for
identification with them. Conscience is the product of the
development of reason and insight. Social spirit is based
more on associative processes; it is the product of his capacity
for being influenced, and having his attitudes shaped, by the
opinion of his fellows. This sentiment is a new and distinct
psychological structure in man which serves to reinforce his
will to justice. Thus his susceptibility to opinion is made
to support rather than efface his moral self. Law is an expression of this self, but social spirit is the creation of the
law.

The institutions which constitute the political machine
are logical implications of Rousseau's view of human nature
and dynamics. Man is a contradictory creature, an amalgam
of moral purpose and bias. Provided he is autonomous, he
can avoid domination by vanity. If he also limits the scope
of moral and political deliberation, he can evade the corrupting influence of self-interest. Rousseau designs a system of
institutions that forces men to make their own moral judgments. In the legislative process each must express his own
opinion as to what justice and the general welfare require.
Personal bias is present in the judgment of each, but through
group deliberation man's will for justice achieves valid ex-

[17] *Ibid.*, Book I, ch. 8.   [18] *Ibid.*

pression. This is guaranteed by restriction of legislation to matters of common concern, which makes it to man's interest to be just. Given creation of a body of just law, man's social sentiment emerges as the keystone of his psychological organization. He remains a contradictory creature, but now his moral rather than his selfish desires are dominant. Thus the general will becomes self-sustaining. Liberty and equality as the goals of legislation have men's positive support, and continued exercise of independent judgment is thereby ensured.

Execution of the general will is the function of government. The government is the agent of the people, "an intermediate body set up between the subjects and the Sovereign, to secure their mutual correspondence, charged with the execution of the laws and the maintenance of liberty, both civil and political." [19] Law is the expression of the general will and can, therefore, be made only by the people. That only the people may make law "does not mean that the commands of the rulers cannot pass for general wills, so long as the Sovereign, being free to oppose them, offers no opposition." [20] In the performance of its primary function the government may create subordinate legislation.

Rousseau fears that the government will tend to subvert the general will because of the biases of its members. "In the government, each member is first of all himself, then a magistrate, and then a citizen—in an order exactly the reverse of what the social system requires." [21] The result of bias is that "sooner or later the prince must inevitably suppress the Sovereign and break the social treaty." [22] Gradually the government deviates from the law, becomes tyrannical, and places the people in a position of personal dependence.

How may this fatal tendency be counteracted? Rousseau's

[19] *Ibid.*, Book III, ch. 1. [20] *Ibid.*, Book II, ch. 1.
[21] *Ibid.*, Book III, ch. 2. [22] *Ibid.*, Book III, ch. 10.

answer consists in the institution of the periodical assembly of the people. The government must be made accountable to the sovereign. At these meetings the authority of the government is automatically suspended, and the people sit in judgment on it.

The opening of these assemblies, whose sole object is the maintenance of the social treaty, should always take the form of putting two propositions that may not be suppressed, which should be voted on separately.

The first is: "Does it please the Sovereign to preserve the present form of government?"

The second is: "Does it please the people to leave its administration in the hands of those who are actually in charge of it?" [23]

The first question is addressed to the sovereign because it constitutes a general matter, one upon which the general will may express itself. The second is addressed to the people, not to the sovereign, because the composition of the government is a particular matter since specific individuals are involved. Their dismissal from office is the sanction by means of which Rousseau hopes to keep government responsive to the general will.

With the addition of this institution, Rousseau's political system would appear to be complete. He has formulated legitimate conditions of association, designed a political machine to express the general will, established a government to administer the law, and found a way to control that government. Enforcement of accountability through periodical assemblies should be sufficient to keep the government from breaking the "social treaty." The people living under a regime of just law should develop social spirit, and the political system should be stable. But Rousseau is not satisfied.

He thinks the weak point in the political system is the

[23] *Ibid.*, Book III, ch. 18.

periodical assembly. Do the people have sufficient social spirit to make this a real check on government, especially if it will make every effort to prevent their meeting? "The people in assembly, I shall be told, is a mere chimera." [24] It may be that the Romans met in assembly every few weeks. But how can the people assemble in a country as large as France? The only real solution to the problem of responsible government, Rousseau thinks, is to have small states. This is impracticable. "If the State cannot be reduced to the right limits, there remains still one resource; this is, to allow no capital, to make the seat of government move from town to town, and to assemble by turn in each the Provincial Estates of the country." [25] But even this form of assembly does not appear practicable to Rousseau, and for two reasons: the government is bound to resist any assembly of the people, and the people are not likely to have sufficient public spirit to overcome this resistance. "When the citizens are greedy, cowardly, and pusillanimous, and love ease more than liberty, they do not long hold out against the redoubled efforts of the government; and thus, as the resisting force incessantly grows, the sovereign authority ends by disappearing, and most cities fall and perish before their time." [26]

Rousseau considers the possibility of obtaining responsible government by the device of a representative legislature, but only to dismiss it. The very idea of representation is founded in lack of social spirit. "The lukewarmness of patriotism, the activity of private interest, the vastness of States, conquest and the abuse of government suggested the method of having deputies or representatives of the people in the national assemblies." [27] The decisive objection against representation is that the general will may be expressed only by the people. "Sovereignty, for the same reason as makes it inalienable, cannot be represented; it lies

24 *Ibid.*, Book III, ch. 12. 25 *Ibid.*, Book III, ch. 13.
26 *Ibid.*, Book III, ch. 14. 27 *Ibid.*, Book III, ch. 15.

essentially in the general will, and will does not admit of representation: it is either the same, or other; there is no intermediate possibility." [28] The people may no more have representatives than they may agree to delegate authority to make law to the government. In either case they would place themselves in a position of personal dependence.

Rousseau affirms that successful expression of the general will should lead to the requisite intensity of public spirit to make the periodical assembly effective. But man's alienation from his civic responsibilities always remains a danger. "As soon as any man says of the affairs of the State, *What does it matter to me?* the State may be given up for lost." [29] He appears to have thought that a solution to the problem of responsible government could be found in federation. "I will show later on how the external strength of a great people may be combined with the convenient polity and good order of a small State." [30] But he never develops this suggestion. Rather his thinking takes a different turn. The impasse of his political system is the matter of social spirit. Its stability requires more intense social sentiment than the system naturally and spontaneously generates in men.

28 *Ibid.*   29 *Ibid.*
30 *Ibid.*

Chapter

6

INTENSIFICATION
OF SOCIAL
SENTIMENT

WE HAVE SO FAR been concerned mainly with Rousseau's view of the institutional requirements of human nature, with the social and political institutions required by human dynamics for the realization of man's moral potentialities and his achievement of goodness. Attention now must shift to the human requirements of Rousseau's political system, to the attitudes men must have if that system is to be stable. He thinks stability demands more intense social sentiment than arises spontaneously in men living under guidance of the general will. Because of personal and group biases in government, this intensity of feeling is insufficient to guarantee the integrity of the law and the contract. Therefore, Rousseau attempts to strengthen men's social sentiment. Their attitude toward civic obligations must be made stronger if the state is not to degenerate into a tyrannical regime, the members of which are in a position of personal dependence. The question is whether his methods for intensifying social sentiment are consistent with both his view of human dynamics and his moral ideals.

Social sentiment may take the form either of social interest or social spirit. The distinction is between growth in man of interest in others and concern for their welfare, and growth of group feeling, a sense of unity with and attachment to others. The intense forms of these attitudes are, respectively, humanitarianism and patriotism.

Social interest and social spirit are acquired by men in essentially different ways. According to Rousseau's theory of human nature, there are two processes by which attitudes are acquired. Attitudes may be a function of rational insight. When men mature in accordance with the pattern of their autonomous tendencies, they naturally and necessarily acquire certain attitudes such as conscience. Social interest and a humanitarian outlook are also attitudes which depend on the development and exercise of reason.

Attitudes may also be acquired by a process of mutual conditioning in which men respond to one another's opinions. Vanity is such an attitude, and so is social spirit. In an improperly organized society men become vain and strive to surpass each other. In a society where the general will is operative men acquire social spirit. They become habituated to life in such a society and acquire a positive attitude toward its laws and institutions.

These two processes are not in themselves necessarily incompatible, although they may become so if deliberate intensification of social spirit is undertaken in order to offset men's hedonistic tendencies and to obtain responsible government. Indeed, these processes may supplement each other. Presence of social spirit, spontaneously acquired, does not preclude men's being conscientious. These attitudes reinforce each other. But the process by which social spirit is acquired may displace entirely social interest by depriving man of his capacity for rational insight. Intense social spirit —namely, patriotism—based on deliberate conditioning of man, may so weaken his capacity for rational insight that he is deprived not only of conscience and social interest but also of moral freedom. In this case, associative processes do not supplement those based on insight but actually eliminate them from man's nature.

Social interest is the attitude the formation of which is described in *Émile*. Émile's interest in his fellows and his concern for their welfare are based mainly on his capacity for sympathy. Pride does enter into it in so far as Rousseau affirms that full realization of his moral potentialities requires extension of his self-love to others. Like his conscience, Émile's interest in his fellows is primarily the product of increased understanding of himself and his relations to them. The emotion mainly involved, sympathy, is a rather dispassionate type of emotion, and social interest is primarily rational. It is grounded in man's love for himself in the sense of self-respect and is essentially a sympathetic respect for others; as such it is in accord with the dictates of reason and conscience.

Social interest is the form which social sentiment takes in the "natural man," the man who lives for himself primarily, such as Emile. He has not entered into society or become a member of a group. Consequently he has little or no feeling of identification with, or attachment to, any particular group of men. His social sentiment is focused on men in general, on humanity. Social spirit is the form of social sentiment appropriate to the citizen, the man who is a member of a state. Rousseau says:

The natural man lives for himself; he is the unit, the whole, dependent only on himself and on his like. The citizen is but the numerator of a fraction, whose value depends on its denominator; his value depends upon the whole, that is, on the community. Good social institutions are those best fitted to make a man unnatural, to exchange his independence for dependence, to merge the unit in the group, so that he no longer regards himself as one, but as part of the whole, and is only conscious of the common life.[1]

Social spirit is the attitude the development of which is analyzed in *The Social Contract*. It is seen as the emotional

1 Rousseau, *Émile*, p. 7.

consequence of life in a society based on self-government and justice. It is less the product of reason and insight than of habit and association. To be sure, it has a sympathetic component, but it is primarily the result of extension of self-love to others, of associating the idea of one's own good with theirs. Social spirit has its focus in the group rather than on humanity in general, and arises less from an understanding of one's self and one's relations to others than from habitual emotional involvement with them. Social interest is natural in that it is the outcome of the development of man's autonomous tendencies. Even when spontaneous, social spirit is more an artificial, a created attitude, the product of man's responsiveness to opinion. Social interest is grounded on insight, social spirit on associative processes. The latter is more in accord with the requirements of the political system.

Rousseau says social interest and social spirit cannot co-exist in the same person. "He who would preserve the supremacy of natural feelings in social life knows not what he asks. Ever at war with himself, hesitating between his wishes and his duties, he will be neither a man nor a citizen." [2] A man's natural interest in and concern for the welfare of others cannot be allowed to interfere with his feeling of obligation to his group. It is this intense but limited feeling of attachment and identification that differentiates the citizen from the "natural man." In his *First Letter from the Mountain,* Rousseau says: "Patriotism and humanity are . . . two virtues incompatible in their energy, and especially in an entire people. The legislator who would like them both will obtain neither one nor the other. This accordance has never come to pass, it never will, because it is contrary to nature, and because one cannot give two objects to the same feeling." [3] Therefore, sentiment in an intense form must

[2] *Ibid.,* p. 8.

[3] Rousseau, *First Letter from the Mountain,* in C. E. Vaughan, ed., *The*

be either a patriotic or a humanitarian attitude. The one attitude excludes existence of the other.

Our purpose in this analysis of Rousseau's view of social sentiment is to show that if he thinks political life requires intensity of group feeling sufficient to preclude existence of social interest, then it follows that political life involves violation of man's moral potentialities. Man cannot be both a completely moral being and a good citizen. Political life necessarily involves limitation of his ethical development. Does it involve more than just limitation? Achievement of political stability may seem to call for methods of intensifying group feeling which in themselves endanger man's moral autonomy.

Rousseau recommends that men live in small states. He says:

It is necessary in some degree to confine and limit our interest and compassion in order to make it active. Now, as this sentiment can be useful only to those with whom we have to live, it is proper that our humanity should confine itself to our fellow-citizens, and should receive a new force because we are in the habit of seeing them, and by reason of the common interest which unites them. It is certain that the greatest miracles of virtue have been produced by patriotism: this fine and lively feeling, which gives to the force of self-love all the beauty of virtue, lends it an energy which, without disfiguring it, makes it the most heroic of all passions.[4]

In a small state intense social spirit would arise spontaneously. Sympathy and self-love fuse into patriotic sentiment and attitudes. In so far as this intensity of feeling arises spontaneously there would seem to be no threat to moral autonomy. Indeed, transformation of self-love into social

---

Political Writings of Jean-Jacques Rousseau, II, 172, n. 2. Author's translation.

4 Rousseau, *A Discourse on Political Economy*, in *The Social Contract and Discourses*, trans. G. D. H. Cole, p. 301. All references to this *Discourse* are to Cole's translation.

spirit through its fusion with sympathy is a condition of the release of moral potentialities. The citizens may not be humanitarians, but they make up in depth for what they lack in breadth of feeling.

The second way in which Rousseau envisages intensification of group feeling is education or, rather, indoctrination for citizenship. In the *Discourse on Political Economy* he says:

There can be no patriotism without liberty, no liberty without virtue, no virtue without citizens; create citizens, and you have everything you need; without them, you will have nothing but debased slaves, from the rulers of the State downwards. To form citizens is not the work of a day; and in order to have men it is necessary to educate them when they are children.[5]

Citizens are made not born. Education for citizenship must begin in childhood. What this involves may be found in Rousseau's *Considerations on the Government of Poland,* where he says, "It is education that must give souls a national formation, and direct their opinions and tastes in such a way that they will be patriotic by inclination, by passion, by necessity." [6] To accomplish this Rousseau recommends instruction and, particularly, games which will enhance the children's responsiveness to the opinion of their fellows. They should become accustomed "at an early age to rules, to equality, to fraternity, to competition, to living under the eyes of their fellow-citizens and to desiring public approbation." [7] This education lays the foundation for "the system of government which . . . seems to me to be capable of bringing patriotism and its attendant virtues to the highest possible degree of intensity." [8] Here the Aristotelian element in Rousseau's thinking becomes most

5 *Ibid.,* p. 307.
6 Rousseau, *Considerations on the Government of Poland,* in *Rousseau: Political Writings,* trans. Frederick Watkins, p. 176. All references to this work are to Watkins' translation.
7 *Ibid.,* p. 179.   8 *Ibid.,* p. 169.

pronounced. "I should wish that, by honors and public rewards, all the patriotic virtues should be glorified." [9]   In practice, "this is to arrange things so that every citizen will feel himself to be constantly under the public eye . . . all shall be so dependent on public esteem that nothing can be done, nothing acquired, no success obtained without it." [10] These statements should be read in the light of Rousseau's assertion in his *Constitutional Project for Corsica* that "the great springs of human conduct come down, on close examination, to two, pleasure and vanity; and what is more, if you subtract from the first all that appertains to the second, you will find in the last analysis that everything comes down to practically pure vanity." [11]   Education for citizenship means to Rousseau deliberate heightening of man's prideful feeling so that he will respond more readily to the opinion and the approval of his fellows.   His social sentiment is to be intensified by stimulating his vanity.   Civil education involves also indoctrination in the values Rousseau thinks appropriate to human nature, justice and fraternity.   The citizens are to win one another's approval by pursuit of these values and in service to the community.   Economic incentives and materialistic values are to be depreciated.

This type of education differs markedly from that described in *Émile*.   In civic education Rousseau seeks deliberately to inculcate moral attitudes so that people will be disposed to feel emotions of obligation and approval in response to appropriate judgments.   Their ethical beliefs and feelings are built into them.   In *Émile* he emphasized the role of personal insight and experience in the development of moral attitudes.   He now relies on indoctrination, imitation, and emulation for their formation.   Moreover,

[9] *Ibid.*, p. 170.   [10] *Ibid.*, p. 244.
[11] Rousseau, *Constitutional Project for Corsica*, in *Rousseau: Political Writings*, trans. Frederick Watkins, p. 325.   All references to this work are to Watkins' translation.

he departs from his conception of the right way for human beings to be brought to maturity. Instead of being retarded, pridefulness is cultivated from the very beginning of man's life. It is not a matter of extending residual self-love to others in order to release moral potentialities. Rather the feeling of self-love is deliberately enhanced to make man more sensitive to the pressure of group approval and disapproval. Children are initiated into a life of mutual surveillance.

Rousseau now advocates exposure of children to the force of authority and opinion, a technique for forming attitudes that he explicitly renounced in *Émile* on the ground that it is incompatible with development of reason, moral insight, and conscience. True, he uses the pridefulness so engendered to reinforce men's commitment to certain values, justice and the general welfare, and to divert them from materialism. But such use of pride, on the basis of his own psychological principles, strikes not only at man's capacity for social interest but also at his capacity for moral independence and deliberation in so far as these are based on the exercise of reason and the consultation of conscience. It precludes the formation of moral attitudes through insight and experience on the basis of man's autonomous tendencies. Even if pride is focused on values that men would think desirable through use of their own reason, even if they are inculcated with attitudes that would have arisen through rational insight, they still have been deprived of their moral freedom and dignity. They lack the capacity for inner determination. They do not make moral and value judgments. They have been conditioned to respond to pressure from their group.

Only if these different methods do not necessarily produce different results can it be said that Rousseau's education for patriotism does not involve violation of man's moral potentialities. If circumstances differ it may even be the case that a different method is required to attain the same results. Émile is protected against environmental influences that would tend to develop his egoistic tendencies. Moreover, when his social emotions appear, Rousseau attempts directly to foster their development. In the case of Polish children possibly more drastic measures are required to neutralize their selfish impulses and release their productive tendencies. Conceivably some intense degree of group feeling is essential to their achievement of insight into the needs of their fellows. Both methods of education would then produce men who have the attitudes and seek the values appropriate to their nature. But Rousseau does think, as we have seen, that the consequence of deliberate intensification of group feeling is to make a person incapable of humanitarian feeling. More importantly, it seems that the kind of social conditioning to which the Polish children are to be exposed certainly weakens, and likely destroys, their capacity for moral autonomy. Even if the attitudes formed in them are later seen by them to be appropriate to their situation, the fact remains that according to Rousseau's own conception of human dynamics their capacity to exercise their own reason will have been stultified. We must conclude, therefore, that for Rousseau different methods necessarily produce different psychological and moral results. Essentially different types of character structures are the outcome of his two educational proposals. The method of *Émile* produces a person of independence capable of making and acting on his own judgments, the other a person who responds and conforms to group judgments in an automaton-like manner.

The third method by which Rousseau seeks to intensify social sentiment is his proposal in *The Social Contract* that the sovereign establish a civil religion. "There is . . . a purely civil profession of faith of which the Sovereign should fix the articles, not exactly as religious dogmas, but as social sentiments without which a man cannot be a good citizen or a faithful subject." [12]   He says:

The dogmas of civil religion ought to be few, simple, and exactly worded, without explanation or commentary. The existence of a mighty, intelligent and beneficent Divinity, possessed of foresight and providence, the life to come, the happiness of the just, the punishment of the wicked, the sanctity of the social contract and the laws: these are its positive dogmas. Its negative dogmas I confine to one, intolerance, which is a part of the cults we have rejected.[13]

The purpose of the civic religion is to increase public spiritedness. "It matters very much to the community that each citizen should have a religion. That will make him love his duty." [14] Religion controls men's prideful tendencies by diverting them away from material interests toward group satisfactions. Without religion man is likely to be dominated by selfishness. "It remains to be seen whether philosophy, safely enthroned, could control successfully man's petty vanity, his self-interest, his ambition, all the lesser passions of mankind, and whether it would practice that sweet humanity which it boasts of, pen in hand." [15]   Moral enlightenment without theological sanctions, Rousseau fears, might allow man's moral impulses to wither. His sense of obligation to his community needs support from religious belief.

The difficulty with other kinds of religion is either that they do not develop social spirit, or if they do, it is not the right kind. Rousseau objects to Roman Christianity on the ground that it destroys social unity. "All that destroys social unity is worthless; all institutions that set man in contradic-

[12] Rousseau, *The Social Contract*, Book IV, ch. 8.
[13] *Ibid.*   [14] *Ibid.*
[15] Rousseau, *Émile*, p. 276, n. 1.

tion to himself are worthless." [16] National religion "makes a people bloodthirsty and intolerant." [17] The trouble with "the religion of man or Christianity" is that "so far from binding the hearts of the citizens to the state, it has the effect of taking them away from all earthly things. I know of nothing more contrary to the social spirit." [18] Lacking social spirit, the true Christian ignores his civic duties and consequently is easily made the victim of a tyrant. He is at the mercy of a "single self-seeker." [19] "Christianity preaches only servitude and dependence. Its spirit is so favorable to tyranny that it always profits by such a régime." [20] Social sentiment in the Christian takes the form of humanitarianism, not patriotism. Rousseau says in his *First Letter from the Mountain,* "Although far from taxing the pure Gospel with being pernicious to society, I do find it in some way too sociable, embracing too much of the human race, for a system of law which ought to be exclusive; inspiring humanity rather than patriotism, and tending to form men rather than citizens." [21] These passages show that Rousseau's object in the civil religion is to fuse religious and patriotic feelings into a single intense feeling of civic devotion and obligation. He desires to instill in people an attitude of alert and energetic concern for the fate of their fellows and country.

Rousseau's ideas about how to intensify social sentiment —a small state, civic education, and civil religion—are all born of his fear that his political machine will not generate sufficient group feeling and devotion to the public interest to prevent government from becoming tyrannical. Only a

---

16 Rousseau, *The Social Contract,* Book IV, ch. 8.
17 *Ibid.*   18 *Ibid.*
19 *Ibid.*   20 *Ibid.*
21 Rousseau, *First Letter from the Mountain,* in C. E. Vaughan, ed., *The Political Writings of Rousseau,* II, 172. Author's translation.

patriotic citizenry can accomplish this. If the people are materialistic and self-interested, they will not act to resist encroachments on their liberties. All three methods involve limitation of man's moral development. The patriotic citizen is not a humanitarian. Neither, it may be said, is he an aggressive nationalist. His attitude is not warlike but civic. What Rousseau does, at the very least, is to deprive man of his capacity for social interest in order to obtain government responsive to the general will.

The proposal for a small state does not appear to involve danger to man's moral freedom. A man may be concerned only with the welfare of his group, identify himself with that group, and also be autonomous. The civic education does threaten individuality. The methods by which intense patriotic feeling is developed and sustained impair man's reasoning power and deprive him of his capacity for self-determination. Equally serious is the recommendation for a civil religion. Here authority is used to forbid exercise of reason as to the validity of the dogmas. Even if acceptance of the dogmas should be dictated by man's conscience, according to Rousseau's theory of human nature such use of authority must certainly impair the individual's capacity to reason. To subject men to the force of opinion in this way is to deprive them of their moral autonomy. Since expression of the general will depends on individuals' exercise of independent judgment, it too must be hindered by these proposals.

It is failure to solve the problem of responsible government that leads Rousseau to propose measures that would violate man's moral potentialities. Only intense group feeling can prevent tyranny. Since the requisite intensity of feeling does not arise spontaneously except in a small state, Rousseau undertakes to create it. His search for ways to do this ends in destruction of moral freedom.

The unifying aim of Rousseau's moral and political theory

is control of man's tendency toward prideful materialism. This constellation of attitudes and values produces dissatisfaction.   Men deceive one another into thinking otherwise. They may and often do become vain self-seekers.   But only justice and goodness can fully satisfy creatures constituted as they are.

There are two methods, essentially different, by which Rousseau tries to achieve his aim of controlling prideful materialism, and these correspond to his distinction between "natural" and "social" man.   By educating man in accordance with the natural unfolding of his capacities, his potentialities for reason and conscience may be realized.   He may become a self-determining being who relies upon his inner sources of direction.   Pridefulness may thus be kept from becoming his governing orientation.   It remains as an unconscious bias, and as such, merely a hindrance to moral deliberation and action.   Or instead of mitigating and evading pride, it may be used.   This requires intensifying pride, detaching it from materialistic ambitions, and converting it into patriotism by focusing it on the nation.   An appropriate religion facilitates this process.   Social man, the citizen as distinguished from natural man, lives through and for his group.   Neither is a prideful materialist, and so they differ from the men Rousseau thought he saw around him, but their characters are not alike.   The natural man is independent, while social man lacks inner direction and is highly sensitive to the opinion of his fellows.

These two methods are based on the psychological principles which Rousseau thinks determine how men acquire attitudes and values.   They do this in two essentially different ways.   Rational insight into human nature and human relations produces the structure of attitudes called conscience and social interest.   Together, reason and conscience give man knowledge of the values appropriate to his nature.   Or attitudes and values may be acquired through processes of

conditioning and association. In the first case, it is essential
that pride be minimized so that man may develop and rely
on his own capacities for social understanding and value
appraisal. In the other, cultivation of pride is essential to
increase his responsiveness to group approval and disapproval. His attitudes and values are created through indoctrination and sustained by social pressure.

The question arises whether it is psychologically possible
for both methods to be used. Clearly not, since one involves
decreasing and the other increasing man's pridefulness. The
methods are essentially alternatives. Use of the second in
so far as it involves indoctrination endangers man's capacity
for moral deliberation. Even if pride is associated with, and
focused on, values that man would adhere to on the basis of
rational insight, still his moral freedom and dignity have
been destroyed. Subordination of materialistic and self-interested tendencies to concern for welfare of the group by
intensifying social sentiment strikes at man's individuality
and independence. Under the influence of patriotic feeling,
he does not make his own moral and value judgments. His
attitude toward his fellows disposes him automatically to
respond emotionally to their judgments. A person cannot
be trained both to respond to his group and to exercise his
own judgment.

Robert M. MacIver says, "The criterion of individuality
is not how far each is divergent from the rest but how far
each, in his relations to others, acts autonomously, acts in
his own consciousness, and with his own interpretation, of
the claims of others on himself." [22] Rousseau's "natural"
man, Émile, meets this criterion, but his "social" man, the
intensely patriotic and conformist citizen, does not.

In his discourses on *The Arts and Sciences* and *Inequality*,
Rousseau sees man a vain creature, materialistic, dependent
on opinion. Vanity corrupts his reason, stills his conscience.

[22] MacIver, *Society: A Textbook of Sociology,* p. 47.

It is the source of his moral perversion and failure, the cause of his dissatisfaction.   In *Émile,* Rousseau shows how man may become autonomous, acquire reason and conscience, and avoid enslavement to his group.   In *The Social Contract,* he attempts to use both of the ways in which man acquires attitudes and values.   To obtain reliable moral deliberation, an enlightened general will, he seeks to preserve man's autonomy.   He designs a political system which evokes man's reason and conscience and arouses in him social spirit.   So far the psychological principles of transformation and association supplement each other.   Then the latter displaces the former in Rousseau's thinking.   To secure political liberty and responsibility, man is subjected to authority and opinion because he is not spontaneously sufficiently public spirited. Discharge of his social responsibilities demands intensification of social sentiment.

In his work on Poland, Rousseau gives up the effort to attain his twin ideals of moral autonomy and responsibility, and seeks to attain the latter alone.   By enhancing man's pride and subjecting him to opinion, he sacrifices autonomy to the achievement of an unthinking responsibility.   An attempt at justification of this decision may be found in the following passage from his *Constitutional Project for Corsica:*

Opinion which lays great store by frivolous objects produces vanity; but that which lights on objects intrinsically great and beautiful produces pride.   You can thus render a people either proud or vain, depending on the choice of the objects to which you direct its judgments.

Pride is more natural than vanity, since it consists in deriving self-esteem from truly estimable goods; whereas vanity, by giving value to that which is valueless, is the work of prejudices.[23]

This distinction between vanity and pride is irrelevant so far as moral freedom and dignity are concerned.   Patriotism may be better than materialism, but man remains an autom-

23 Rousseau, *Constitutional Project for Corsica,* p. 326.

aton who pursues the right values and fulfils his obligations without knowing why.   His tendency to become prideful and materialistic has been overcome at the expense of his individuality.

Why is it that Rousseau comes to sacrifice moral autonomy to responsibility or, rather, the substance of both to the appearance of the latter?   There is a tendency in his thinking tacitly to identify moral and political liberty.   If the former consists in imposing rules on one's self, then the latter is certainly a prerequisite to it.   One must be self-governing and not subjected to the authority of another.   But if moral liberty consists in inner determination of these rules, then it may not be identified with political liberty.   Rousseau's patriotic citizens may be politically free, but they are not morally free.

Rousseau tends to identify the two freedoms because he never fully resolves in his thinking the disparity between man's capacity for moral deliberation and his inability to act in accordance with the result of this deliberation.   As E. F. Carritt contends, Rousseau is, part of the time at least, "a psychological hedonist of the altruistic or inconsistent type." [24]   He is trapped between the logical exclusives of psychological hedonism and utilitarianism.   Although man knows he ought to seek the general welfare, although he wants to be just and limit his pursuit of personal good out of regard for the welfare of his fellows, he tends constantly to act to maximize his own happiness.   Justice and benevolence may be all that will really satisfy man, but if he cannot choose them for their own sake, it cannot greatly matter how he is put on the path to them.   If all that is obtainable is happiness, and moral freedom is an illusion, then indoctrination and conditioning are means as good as insight, and possibly better, for getting it.   If man is not morally

[24] Carritt, *Morals and Politics: Theories of Their Relation from Hobbes and Spinoza to Marx and Bosanquet,* p. 68.

free, at least he can be politically free, just in action if not in heart, and public spirited. Indeed, if he is a psychological hedonist, political freedom is the only kind of freedom of which he is capable. If reason and conscience are always overwhelmed by self-interest, there is little point to developing them.

Rousseau's temptation to confuse moral and political freedom is heightened by the fact that he sometimes means by the former man's ability to perform an obligation even though it conflicts with his personal good. Man is free to chose the right, to follow dictates of reason and conscience. At other times, he means that man can overcome his physical and materialistic impulses by imposing legal rules on himself. Now it is true that a person guided by reason and conscience would not, according to Rousseau, be a materialist. But it does not follow that a person who is not a materialist is morally free. He may be a manufactured patriot, politically free and self-governing, but rendered incapable by his education of being morally free.

Confusion is compounded by Rousseau's equation of legality and morality. If moral action is possible only through legal forms, then the temptation is to identify conformity with the law with moral freedom. Through law man achieves self-discipline and justice; but only if the law is in reality self-imposed and not the product of self-destroying social discipline. Unless the law is the expression of the individual's own reason and conscience rather than the result of accentuated responsiveness to others, action in accordance with it cannot be called morally free.

Rousseau does waver between thinking that pride and self-interest tend to corrupt moral judgment and action, and that man can act on no motive other than his personal good. Is moral insight imperfect, or is action determined only by self-interest? Rousseau does not say we can never do our duty, only that perception of it is refracted by bias, and that we tend to drift off from it.   Man is a contradictory creature. "If to put oneself first is an inclination natural to man, and the first sentiment of justice is moreover inborn in the human heart, let those who say man is a simple creature remove these contradictions." [25]   Though it may require great moral effort, man can act on motives other than self-interest.   He cannot, of course, if his conscience is inactive, if he is prideful and vain.   The patriotic citizen must, therefore, be assumed always to act in his own interest as he perceives it.   Responsiveness to the opinion of his fellows ensures that he will seek his interest, not in a narrow materialism, but in the public welfare.   Since he lacks moral freedom and insight, but approves equality and fraternity, whatever will preserve his political freedom is good.   This is the only kind of freedom of which the citizen is capable, and it is essential to the realization of the values to which he has been conditioned.

In terms of his own theory of human nature and dynamics, the means by which Rousseau seeks to achieve and sustain political liberty are incompatible with man's moral freedom. Intensification of social sentiment in the form of patriotism is fatal to his ideals of autonomy and responsibility.   The attitudes required for stability of his political system can be acquired by man only in ways that preclude the release and exercise of his moral capacities.

Our analysis of Rousseau's political theory suggests that Ernst Cassirer is only partly right in saying that Rousseau "was concerned with the dignity of man and with the means of securing and realizing it." [26]   Certainly this is Rousseau's central concern, and it leads him, as Cassirer points out, to the principle that "in the world of the will every one is truly only that which he has made of himself and by himself." [27]

[25] Rousseau, *Émile*, p. 241.
[26] Cassirer, *The Question of Jean-Jacques Rousseau*, trans. Peter Gay, p. 71.
[27] *Ibid.*, p. 124.

Rousseau's ideal of character and personality is the independent yet responsible man. But he does not always hold fast to this ideal. He is capable of sacrificing freedom and dignity to satisfaction in community life and values. In his later work especially, he is all too ready to trade the reality for the appearance of social virtue. Bernard Groethuysen is also right in arguing that "the principle of conscience applies to neither the state of nature nor the social state. It goes beyond natural man and is transcended in its turn by the social ideal." [28] Rousseau's conditioned citizen, although he has no conscience, does pretty much what a man with conscience would do. He is not Rousseau's ideal man, rather he is a man with the attitudes Rousseau thinks required by political life.

There is an unresolved tension in Rousseau's thought between radical Christian emphasis on moral creativity and Platonic willingness to impose order and value on human life at the expense of moral liberty and dignity. This arises from his opposition to prideful materialism combined with his doubt of the possibility of obtaining consistently moral motivation in men. It is the strain of psychological hedonism in his thinking that accounts for Rousseau's final sacrifices of his moral ideals to political freedom and responsibility. He could not steadily quite believe that autonomous men could create and sustain political order. He failed to synthesize the classical and Christian elements in his thinking, and in the attempt to do so was led to blur the distinction between moral and political freedom.

28 Groethuysen, *Jean-Jacques Rousseau,* p. 266. Author's translation.

7

TOTALITARIAN
IMPLICATIONS
LIMITED

IN VIEW OF THE divergent tendencies in his thought, it is not surprising that current appraisals of Rousseau's political theory conflict. Some regard it as fundamentally liberal and democratic while others see totalitarian implications. Typical of the latter opinion is Bertrand Russell's judgment that "Hitler is an outcome of Rousseau; Roosevelt and Churchill, of Locke." [1] Alfred Cobban says, "Dictatorship is both the logical and also the historical consequence of the democratic theory of the General Will." [2] To bring the indictment up to date, note the opinion of A. J. P. Taylor that "Hitler and 'the new democracies' of eastern Europe have both a most respectable ancestry; both represent different forms of the General Will, which Rousseau invented." [3] These views are perhaps best summed up in J. L. Talmon's statement:

Rousseau's sovereign is the externalized general will, and . . . stands for essentially the same as the natural harmonious order. In marrying this concept with the principle of popular sovereignty, and popular self-expression, Rousseau gave rise to totalitarian democracy.[4]

There is hardly a disaster of the modern world which is not traced by someone to Rousseau.

[1] Russell, *A History of Western Philosophy* p. 685.
[2] Cobban, *The Crisis of Civilization*, p. 67.
[3] Taylor, "Totalitarianism (I)," in *The Western Tradition: A Series of Talks Given in the B. B. C. European Programme*, p. 66.
[4] Talmon, *The Rise of Totalitarian Democracy*, p. 43.

Others consider his political theory essentially liberal. Robert Derathé emphasizes his belief in the importance of reason in social life. Ernst Cassirer and Bernard Groethuysen both call attention to his recognition of man's need for autonomy. Ernest Hunter Wright says, "The idea that man must be perfected by his reason in accordance with his nature runs through all of Rousseau's work and gives it an essential unity." [5] According to G. D. H. Cole, "Rousseau's cardinal contribution to political theory is his assertion that will and not force is the only legitimate basis for social obligation, and that the General Will, present in every citizen, provides the only nexus between men that is consistent with reason and capable of reconciling the claims of society with those of personal freedom and self-expression." [6] A. D. Lindsay holds that the idea of a general will implies that "the spirit of the common life is the sovereign principle by which legislation should be guided." [7] Especially noteworthy as a liberal interpretation of Rousseau's thought is Hendel's *Jean-Jacques Rousseau: Moralist*.[8] Hendel argues that Rousseau's respect for freedom is central to his moral and political theory.

Rousseau's interpreters tend to fasten on one or the other divergent tendency in his thought. Emphasis on his concern for moral creativity makes Rousseau a liberal. If his willingness to impose order and value on human life is brought to the fore, he becomes a totalitarian. This is the fate of a thinker whose psychological theory tempts him to seek essentially Christian ends through classical means. The purpose of this chapter is to disentangle the totalitarian from the liberal elements in Rousseau's political theory with a view to appraising the contention that it is fundamentally totalitarian, that it logically implies dictatorship and the depreciation of individual freedom.

[5] Wright, *The Meaning of Rousseau*, p. 32.
[6] Cole, "Rousseau's *Social Contract*," in *Persons and Periods: Studies*, p. 259.
[7] Lindsay, *The Modern Democratic State*, I, 242.
[8] Charles William Hendel, *Jean-Jacques Rousseau: Moralist*, 2 vols.

The implication of dictatorship may seem plausible because of Rousseau's concept of the "legislator." His role is to design and secure popular acceptance of the political machine. Rousseau describes him as "the engineer who invents the machine." [9] He is the constitution-maker.

Rousseau's concern with the "legislator" springs from his conviction that the people do not have sufficient grasp of political principles to enable them to establish a sound constitution by themselves. This is the clear implication of his view that men do not understand how their character is developed and transformed by their societies. Moreover, before social spirit appears men are unwilling to make the sacrifices of selfish interests which a sound constitution involves. In effect, the people are incompetent to make basic social and political reforms. They are at the mercy of destructive social processes, the inertia of which is so great that only a striking personality who has their confidence can put the general will into operation. If men are dominated by selfish tendencies, if materialism is their operative ideal, they are trapped in social processes over which they have no control and which function to prevent the realization of their moral capacities. In these situations the "legislator" finds both his task and his opportunity. Either construction or reconstruction of the political and social order is called for.

His task is difficult. If design of the political machine is faulty it will operate to stultify men. He must select the appropriate time for his work. "The moment chosen is one of the surest means of distinguishing the work of the legislator from that of the tyrant." [10] During periods of stress such as war, famine, or sedition the "legislator" cannot successfully perform his function. These qualifications of knowledge and purpose have rarely been met. They ex-

9 Rousseau, *The Social Contract*, Book II, ch. 7.
10 *Ibid.*, Book II, ch. 10.

clude from the position the modern dictators who came to power in times of social turmoil. Robespierre and Hitler are not candidates for the job. Alexander Hamilton and James Madison do meet Rousseau's criteria; and Rousseau himself does, notably in his plans for the governments of Poland and Corsica.

Was Napoleon a "legislator"? According to John Holland Rose, he was not only a "legislator" but also acted on principles laid down by Rousseau. "Mankind was to be saved by law, society being levelled down and levelled up until the ideals of Lycurgus were attained." [11] Although Napoleon's purpose may qualify him for the job, his lack of understanding of human nature and political processes serves to disqualify him. Rose says, "He never completely understood religion, or the enthusiasm which it can evoke; neither did he ever fully realize the complexity of human nature, the many-sidedness of social life, and the limitations that beset the action even of the most intelligent lawmaker." [12] Even though he has to his credit the Code Napoléon, this is offset by the limitless personal ambition which led to his downfall. Napoleon fails to meet the requirements of a Rousseauist "legislator." He was neither sufficiently disinterested nor foresighted, and, as Rose points out, his political insight was defective. Furthermore, his grandiose schemes were anything but in accord with Rousseau's ideals. As John Plamenatz says:

If ever a political society existed that looked like a copy (though a very imperfect one) of the ideal state described by Rousseau, it was not the revolutionary France of the Jacobins but the Paris Commune of 1871. The Commune was a small political society, simple, equalitarian and democratic; it respected property, made provision for the poor, disliked the wealthy, mistrusted all

11 Rose, *The Life of Napoleon I: Including New Materials from the British Official Records*, I, 39.
12 *Ibid.*, I, 19.

authority not directly responsible to the people, and was never dominated by any organized party or any one faction.[13]

Rousseau's "legislator" is no charismatic leader through whom the general will may be expressed. Expression of the general will requires both group effort and individual integrity and is based on a process of dynamic interaction. The participants in this process may achieve consensus. If they do, it is a dynamic consensus, one which emerges from mutual adjustment of their ideas and purposes. Each must be free to express his own opinion as to what justice and the general welfare require. The general will, therefore, cannot be interpreted and imposed on a people by a dictator. Indeed, presence of a dictator would deprive them of their personal independence, the "key to the working of the political machine." [14]   Freedom, both moral and political, is essential to the very existence of a general will. The "legislator's" essential task is to discern and establish the conditions of freedom.

Failure to appreciate its dynamic quality mars J. L. Talmon's account of Rousseau's general will, and enables him to argue that it is the conceptual basis for modern totalitarian democracy. This is "a dictatorship resting on popular enthusiasm. . . . In so far as it is a dictatorship based on ideology and the enthusiasm of the masses, it is the outcome . . . of the synthesis between the eighteenth-century idea of the natural order and the Rousseauist idea of popular fulfilment and self-expression." [15]   Talmon's equation of the general will with "popular fulfilment and self-expression" neglects its dynamic aspects. Support for his view may be found in Rousseau's proposals for intensifying patriotic sentiment, but this is a different matter. They are designed not so much to ensure the expression of the general will as

13 Plamenatz, *The Revolutionary Movement in France, 1815-71*, p. xi.
14 Rousseau, *The Social Contract*, Book i, ch. 7.
15 Talmon, *The Rise of Totalitarian Democracy*, p. 6.

to maintain it, and, as we have argued, are incompatible with the former. Rousseau's general will cannot be treated as popular desire for justice and happiness without regard for its dynamic method of expression. This is "as if you were to turn harmony into mere unison, or to reduce a theme to a single beat." [16] Moreover, Rousseau was sceptical of the eighteenth-century idea of "the natural order." This is a Physiocratic concept, foreign to his belief that there is a persistent tendency toward moral and political disorder. On this point, Rousseau is a Platonist not a Physiocrat.[17] The natural drift of society is toward tyranny based on prideful materialism. The creation and maintenance of order requires both individual insight and group effort expressed through the political machine in the form of the general will.

Talmon overlooks the dynamic aspects of the general will because he gives Rousseau's conception of freedom a purely political interpretation. Rousseau, "when speaking of man's dignity and freedom, means the absence of personal dependence, in other words, equality." [18] He adheres to the "ancient idea of liberty" which "connoted above all the active and equal participation of the citizen in the shaping of the sovereign will, in the exercise of active citizenship rights; not so much his freedom, as his dignity as a member of the sovereign." [19] Rousseau does tend to confuse moral and political freedom, and this is certainly a cardinal deficiency of his thought. But "absence of personal dependence" does not mean only political liberty and equality. It has moral implications as well. "Absence of personal dependence" is a necessary, although not a sufficient, condition of moral freedom. Rousseau opposes "personal dependence" because

[16] Aristotle, *Politics,* trans. Ernest Barker, p. 62.
[17] See Charles Gide and Charles Rist, *A History of Economic Doctrines, from the Time of the Physiocrats to the Present Day,* pp. 25-31.
[18] Talmon, *The Rise of Totalitarian Democracy,* p. 91.
[19] *Ibid.,* p. 278.

it precludes men's being morally free and able to express the general will. If men have authority and power over one another, they necessarily become vain and prideful. Their selfish tendencies are released, and this deprives them of reason and conscience.

Liberty means to Rousseau not just political equality, as Talmon holds, but also individual autonomy. His aversion to personal dependence cannot be equated with demand for political liberty without doing violence to his psychological and moral theories. Moreover, it robs his concept of the general will of its dynamic quality and its basis in moral independence. Confusion, not fusion, of moral and political liberty is Rousseau's weakness. No doubt he does desire "active and equal participation of the citizen in the shaping of the sovereign will." But this in itself is not inconsistent with his moral freedom. It is so only when combined with subjection to the opinion and surveillance of his patriotic fellows.

Rousseau is thought to frown on freedom of association and multi-group society. Frederick Watkins says the general will "can never be delegated, but must always be exercised by the unorganized mass of the population. These beliefs, which lie at the center of Rousseau's political thought, represent a totalitarian ideal of social integration." [20] It is true that Rousseau thinks expression of the general will cannot be delegated to the government. But this does not imply that the general will may be expressed only by the "unorganized mass of the population." Rousseau does not intend to ban groups from society. This is no necessary implication of his political theory.[21] Expression of the general will requires that no one group have a monopoly of political power and

[20] Watkins, *The Political Tradition of the West: A Study in the Development of Modern Liberalism*, p. 108.

[21] See Rousseau's analysis of the role of groups in society in *A Discourse on Political Economy*, pp. 290-291.

that there be a sufficient number of groups to ensure diversity of views on the common interest.

Rousseau is aware of the multiplication of groups in the social ferment of the eighteenth century.[22] Georges Lefebvre says that "societies of all kinds . . . were founded in great numbers."[23] This took place in a society long dominated by the privileged corporations of the *ancien régime*. In consequence the French attitude toward groups and their place in society is ambivalent. According to Lefebvre, the *Declaration of the Rights of Man* "says nothing of the right of association, not because the Assembly meant to prohibit it purely and simply, for the clubs became one of the most solid pillars in revolutionary organization, but rather because it was inopportune to proclaim a right of association at a time when the clergy was to cease to be a 'body,' and when suppression of property in office was to put an end to the judicial 'bodies' also."[24] No doubt Rousseau shares this ambivalent attitude. But opposition to groups as such is not essential to his theory of the general will. He does envisage a multi-group society, although he is insensitive to the possibility of multiple-group membership. This is not surprising in view of the fact that eighteenth-century society was class-bound.

In A. D. Lindsay's interpretation of Rousseau's political

[22] The new consciousness of individuality, to which Leonard Woolf calls attention, was bound to have such an effect: "Just as a profound change took place in the communal psychology of Europe with regard to happiness between 1700 and 1800, so, too, during the same period there was a profound change in the consciousness of individuality" (*After the Deluge*, I, 242). Robert M. MacIver points out that "the new recognition of the nature of personality and the modern multiplicity of associations go hand in hand" (*The Web of Government*, p. 439).

[23] Lefebvre, *The Coming of the French Revolution*, trans. R. R. Palmer, p. 49. Note also T. S. Ashton's observation on the state of England in the same period: "In the eighteenth century the characteristic instrument of social purpose was not the individual or the State, but the club" (*The Industrial Revolution, 1760-1830*, p. 127).

[24] Lefebvre, *The Coming of the French Revolution*, p. 176.

theory we find still another example of neglect of the dynamic aspects of the general will. According to Lindsay,

> Rousseau could find no person or body of persons who ought to be obeyed—no person, that is, in the ordinary sense of the word. But because he retained the notion of sovereignty, and therefore of a will which was a sufficient source of authority, he found another sort of person to meet his problem, society as a whole . . . no one individual or collection of individuals can be the source of the rightful authority of law. But there is a *moi commun* in society: society has supreme authority over us, for to it we owe all that we are.[25]

Rousseau does retain the notion of sovereignty with its attributes of inalienability, indivisibility, and illimitability. But it may be questioned whether this notion in the sense of a will which is a "sufficient source of authority" plays so important a role in his political theory as Lindsay's statement suggests. Rousseau's references to a *moi commun* are best interpreted in the context of his psychological and moral theories as an attempt to express the idea of a psychological group, the members of which are in dynamic interaction. On this view of Rousseau's meaning, the authority of the general will is based on its being the legal expression of man's moral purpose and desire for justice. The "will of all" is also the will of society but it is without moral authority. The authority of the general will is the authority of just law and not of society as such. Social will alone is not sufficient to validate values. This is the function of reason and conscience.

If we do regard the authority of the general will as the authority of society, it must be recognized that it is society organized in a certain way and making law according to certain procedures, all of which are designed to ensure the reliability of moral and political deliberation. It is society

25 Lindsay, *The Modern Democratic State,* I, 236.

as based on the "social contract" and operating through the "political machine." In this case, the authority of law is derived from the conditions under which it is made, conditions which are designed to ensure that all law is "natural law"—that is, is just. Then Rousseau's conception of the sovereignty of the general will is similar to what Lindsay himself describes as the "sovereignty of the constitution." [26] In either case, the authority of the general will is based on justice and not merely on its being the product of group effort. The contention that it may be discovered and expressed only by society through discussion does not alter its ultimate ground of authority, as, indeed, Lindsay himself admits.[27]

Neglect of the dynamic aspects of Rousseau's general will distorts the nature of the consensus which he thinks men ought to aim at and can achieve. It is not a consensus which may be imposed, which can be described in terms of conformity, or which represents the subordination of individuals to society. Rather it is a dynamic consensus, the validity of which depends on individual autonomy. This form of consensus may hardly be described as an illiberal ideal. Nor can the process by which it may be attained be described as undemocratic. It is thoroughly democratic in its recognition of the value of the contribution which may be made by each and every participant to the expression of the general will.

There is a tension in liberal democratic theory between liberty and equality. Two traditions may be distinguished, one of which emphasizes liberty and the other, equality. According to George H. Sabine, "What tied together liberty and equality in democratic thought was the ideal, common to both traditions, of a society and government formed by the willing coalescence of human beings who could be at

[26] *Ibid.*, ch. 9.　　　　　　　　[27] *Ibid.*, p. 237.

once spontaneous in their behavior and responsible in their dealings with one another." [28]   Although Sabine identifies Rousseau with the tradition which stresses equality, his view of the link between liberty and equality in democratic thought puts perfectly Rousseau's ideal of social integration. So far as this ideal is based on a general will, it requires existence of resilient personalities who can be independent yet considerate of public judgment and concerned with public welfare.

It may still be contended, however, that Rousseau fails to attach sufficient importance to individuals' purposes.   The general will is unlimited.   The sovereign's authority is so great that it constitutes a perpetual threat to the individual's freedom of action.   "Each man alienates, I admit, by the social compact, only such part of his powers, goods and liberty as it is important for the community to control; but it must also be granted that the Sovereign is sole judge of what is important." [29]   Individuals' rights are dissolved in a vague utilitarianism, the scope of which is left for the sovereign to define.

The force of this contention is surely weakened by the consideration that the institutions which Rousseau prescribes for making the general will operative are also limits upon the sovereign.   The sovereign may express itself only after deliberation and only on matters of common concern.   Indeed, the requirement that legislation must apply to all may be too severe a limitation on the competence of the sovereign if men are to obtain their objective of justice for all.   If men's needs are different, justice requires discriminating judgment and this is the very thing the sovereign may not attempt.   In his effort to protect the general will against bias, Rousseau may well have undermined his claim that its

[28] Sabine, "The Two Democratic Traditions," *The Philosophical Review*, LXI (Oct., 1952), 473-74.
[29] Rousseau, *The Social Contract*, Book II, ch. 4.

expression guarantees justice, if we mean by that equal treatment with respect to equally central needs. This requires exercise of discriminating judgment.

In so far as law must apply to all, the sovereign cannot oppress any particular individual or group. It is possible, however, that the sovereign may oppress all individuals, that the people may enmesh themselves in a web of legal constraints and promote justice and welfare at the expense of liberty. Whether this is likely or not depends on the strength of the people's desire for freedom. It is not a necessary implication of the theory of the general will.

Finally, we may point out that Rousseau, far from being a totalitarian, is not even a majoritarian democrat. In expression of the general will, "the more grave and important the questions discussed, the nearer should the opinion that is to prevail approach unanimity." [30] Important decisions cannot be made by bare majorities. This recognition of the rights of minorities is quite in accord with liberal democratic theory. The sovereign's authority depends not on will but on right.

Neither Rousseau's concept of the "legislator" nor his theory of a general will can be described as totalitarian in its implications. He does not arm man against the state with rights inherited from the "state of nature." But it does not follow that he depreciates individual liberty. Expression of the general will requires liberty of opinion and does not preclude liberty of association. There are limits on the scope of the general will which carve out for individuals spheres of action in which they are not controlled by sovereign authority. Each individual has the right to participate in the making of law. Indeed, according to the theory of the general will, law can be made only through a process of discussion to which the individual may make a unique contribution. Rousseau's ideal is that discussion

[30] *Ibid.*, Book IV, ch. 2.

produce consensus. But this is no static concept. He sees consensus as evolving through clash of individual views on the common welfare. So far as his theory of the general will is concerned, Rousseau is no advocate of totalitarian democracy.

The totalitarian aspect of Rousseau's political theory lies in his proposals for intensifying social sentiment. In particular, his proposal for a civil religion is widely regarded as the manifestation of a totalitarian orientation. An exception is G. D. H. Cole, who says that Rousseau's "notion of the relations between Church and State was a denial of all admission of political *pluralism;* but it was not totalitarian. . . . because the underlying purpose was not that of subordinating the individual to the State, but rather that of preserving the final right of the individual against all institutions in the exercise of his fundamental sovereignty." [31] Cole is right in his appraisal of Rousseau's aim. But it does not follow that the proposal is not totalitarian. The purpose of the civil religion may be to preserve man's political freedom, but it is a means which destroys his moral freedom and dignity. This is surely sufficient to make it totalitarian.

Rousseau's attempt deliberately to create patriotic feeling and to subject men to the surveillance of their fellows is the point on which he diverges most sharply from modern liberal democratic theory. Much more than did the classical liberal, the modern liberal recognizes a need for social sentiment. But he doubts whether Rousseau's methods would achieve his end. William Ernest Hocking says, "social cohesion, loyalty, lawfulness are dispositions upon which every social structure depends, but which society cannot directly produce." [32] Social unity and a sense of civic obligation are seen as the outcomes of freedom. Direct attempts to generate social sentiment in men are likely only to create stark

31 Cole, "Rousseau's Political Theory," in *Essays in Social Theory,* p. 125.
32 Hocking, *Human Nature and Its Remaking,* p. 276.

scepticism. Robespierre's effort to establish a kind of civil religion may have been inspired by Rousseau, but its fate bears out the liberal view that growth of social sentiment must be spontaneous if it is to be firm and lasting. According to J. M. Thompson, "The *culte de l'Être Suprême* was never abolished: it simply disappeared." [33] Nothing could make more clear the essential artificiality of a civil religion, especially when we consider that the French Revolution "was sustained by an emotional impulse, a mystical faith in humanity, in the ultimate regeneration of the human race." [34]

Even if social sentiment of the kind that Rousseau envisages could be deliberately created and sustained in men, the modern liberal would question its value. As MacIver says, "The unity is the vehicle, not the subject of values." [35] The Rousseau who stands for individual moral creativity would agree, not so the devotee of patriotism. He has fallen in with man's inveterate tendency to overvalue his group and its life at the expense of individuals. He has come to think that value, like the shape of a circle, is a quality that resides in the whole. Rousseau would have men value their nations without detriment to the welfare of individuals. He does not, like the totalitarians of today, envisage elimination of dissident personalities and groups. Patriotism is always coupled in his mind with devotion to justice, liberty, and fraternity. The difficulty is that the means by which he seeks to secure social unity and sentiment transfer the individual from the center to the circumference of value. Authoritarian means do not achieve liberal ends.

Intensification of social sentiment is not, however, central to Rousseau's political theory. The means by which he seeks

---

[33] Thompson, *The French Revolution*, p. 546.

[34] Carl L. Becker, *The Heavenly City of the Eighteenth-Century Philosophers*, p. 155.

[35] Robert M. MacIver, *The Web of Government*, p. 419.

to achieve this are inconsistent with man's moral autonomy, and hence inconsistent with his theory of the general will. If this is the case, it is difficult to see how manufactured patriotism can be made the core of Rousseau's political teaching. True, he lacks confidence that operation of his political machine will generate sufficient social spirit to sustain responsible government. There is divergence between Rousseau's view of the institutional requirements of human nature and his view of the attitudes that make for stability in the political system. But intensification of social sentiment is not a prerequisite to the release of moral potentialities. It is an emotional support for a device thought necessary to the control of government. Rousseau advocates patriotic education and civil religion not because these are essential to the generation of a general will, but rather because he thinks these essential to keeping government responsive to the general will. These are means, not ends, to Rousseau. If, as seems clear, their effect would be to undermine the moral foundations of the very will to which they are intended to keep government responsive, they are inappropriate means. For this reason, therefore, although intensification of social sentiment is a totalitarian element in Rousseau's political theory, it would be illogical to consider him an essentially totalitarian theorist.

Part Three

ROUSSEAU AND LIBERALISM

Si, quand le peuple suffisamment informé délibère, les citoyens n'avaient aucune communication entre eux, du grand nombre de petites différences résulterait toujours la volonté générale, et la délibération serait toujours bonne. CONTRAT SOCIAL, BOOK II

Chapter

8

NOVELTY
IN HIS VIEW
OF MAN

THE AIM OF THE following chapters is to fix the intellectual coordinates of Rousseau's ideas about man and the state in terms of liberal doctrines. Liberalism as the historical demand for liberty and justice has taken many forms, depending on the social and political circumstances in which it has arisen.[1] We seek only to determine the relation of Rousseau's ideas to its most significant forms, to what J. Roland Pennock calls the "classical pattern of liberal democracy,"[2] namely, the natural-rights philosophy and English utilitarianism; to the philosophy of the Enlightenment; and to "modern liberalism" as defined by Frederick Watkins. He says:

Like its predecessors, modern liberalism believes in the existence of a natural harmony of interests. Under favorable conditions, the natural tendency of reason is to work for the welfare of mankind. This rational harmony does not, however, emerge spontaneously from the operation of class institutions, but as the result of a comprehensive process of political deliberation. Participation in the organized political life of society is a necessary means to the realization of human freedom. This belief is a distinguishing feature of modern liberal thought.[3]

1 See especially Guido de Ruggiero, *The History of European Liberalism;* Harold J. Laski, *The Rise of Liberalism: The Philosophy of a Business Civilization;* and Maurice Cranston, *Freedom: A New Analysis.*
2 Pennock, *Liberal Democracy: Its Merits and Prospects,* p. 18.
3 Watkins, *The Political Tradition of the West,* p. 244.

Our contention is that although Rousseau's political theory differs significantly from that of classical liberalism, his theory of the general will is remarkably similar to the modern liberal doctrine of the deliberative state.

There are novel features in Rousseau's theory of human nature and dynamics, features which distinguish it from the psychological theories of Hobbes and Locke which were inherited by the classical liberal democrats. Because of these, Rousseau does not fit into the classical pattern of liberal democratic thought. The exception to this generalization is his reliance on the principle of association in the attempt to close the gap between psychological hedonism and utilitarianism by intensification of social sentiment. Here there is no difference in psychological principle between Rousseau and a classical liberal like James Mill. Both wish to condition man to do the things they think he ought, although he cannot desire them for themselves. Paradoxically, the totalitarian aspect of Rousseau's political theory is his closest link with classical liberals on the psychological plane. They do not share his enthusiasm for patriotism. But they are, no less than he, prepared to transmute leaden instincts into golden utilitarian conduct through the alchemy of indoctrination. Only when Rousseau considers the possibility of mutability in human motives and thinks processes other than associative are at work in the human mind, does he depart in principle from the psychological theory of classical liberalism.

The classical liberals inherited their psychological theory from Hobbes and Locke. In its novel aspects Rousseau's theory of human nature and dynamics not only differs from but also synthesizes theirs. The purpose of this chapter is to show the nature of this synthesis. The following chapter deals with Rousseau's differences from classical liberalism and explains how these depend on his conception of man. In the concluding chapter, his theory of the general will is shown to be consistent with the doctrine of the deliberative state.

It is not maintained that Rousseau deliberately combines Hobbes's and Locke's ideas about man. No doubt he was influenced by these thinkers, but the nature of this influence is not our concern. Rather we are interested in the logical relation of Rousseau's thought to theirs because of the impact which they had on classical liberals. Furthermore, our concern is with Hobbes's and Locke's psychological theories. Consideration is given also to their political theories, but no more than is essential to an understanding of their views of human nature. It is these that are relevant to the appreciation of Rousseau's differences from classical liberalism.

In historical perspective, Hobbes and Locke each repudiate the classical view of man as a political animal, a creature with potentialities that may be realized only in society. Both also discard the correlative idea that the purpose of the state is development of human character. The doctrine of self-realization is replaced by ethical materialism and political hedonism. No doubt Machiavelli was the first major political theorist to reject the classical view of man and the state. He saw man a creature of immutable motives with only limited capacity for understanding social and political processes. Men "have been, and ever will be, animated by the same passions." [4] He implicitly assumes that the principle of association governs mental processes in his contention that men cannot grasp the nature of the forces at work in their environment and should, therefore, rely on historical example for guidance of conduct. But Machiavelli was preoccupied with analysis of the techniques of power and was not interested in formulating a systematic political theory. It is Hobbes and Locke

---

4 Niccolò Machiavelli, *Discourses on the First Ten Books of Titus Livius,* trans. Christian E. Detmold, in *The Prince and The Discourses,* p. 530.

who present reasoned alternatives to classic views, the former by describing the purpose of the state as the reconciliation of men's interests, the latter as protection of men's natural rights, especially of their right to property.

Hobbes's psychology is based on the twin principles of association and immutability of motives. He thinks all mental phenomena reducible to the motion of bodies. This mechanistic materialism serves as the philosophical basis for both psychological principles. It guarantees immutability of motives and precludes existence of processes other than associative. Man's vaingloriousness, his desire for power and superiority for their own sake, was postulated, however, by Hobbes before he became concerned with philosophical matters.[5] Vaingloriousness attains the status of a fixed motive in man's psychological organization because materialism is fatal to the idea of psychological development in a social environment,[6] an idea shared by the classical philosophers and Rousseau. In the context of Hobbes's philosophy, striving for power and superiority becomes an innate and unchangeable characteristic of human nature. It cannot be, as Rousseau sees it, the result of man's development in a certain kind of social environment. Any modification of this striving depends on associative processes. For it cannot be displaced in man's nature by the emergence of new motives. These aspects of Hobbes's theory of human nature and dynamics above all distinguish it from that held by Rousseau.

According to Hobbes, man wants felicity. This, he says, "is a continual progress of the desire, from one object to another; the attaining of the former, being still but the way to the latter." [7] Men place felicity in the "acquisition of the gross pleasures of the senses, and the things that most

5 See Leo Strauss, *The Political Philosophy of Hobbes: Its Basis and Its Genesis,* trans. Elsa M. Sinclair, ch. 1.

6 See R. G. Collingwood, *The Idea of Nature,* pp. 82ff.

7 Thomas Hobbes, *Leviathan,* p. 63.

immediately conduce thereto." [8]   They are materialists.
But decisive to achievement of felicity is getting the better
of the other fellow.   Because of their desire for superiority,
men "are continually in competition for honour and
dignity." [9]   Man's "joy consisteth in comparing himself with
other men." [10]   Each finds his satisfaction in disappointments
of others and desires to be the recipient of steady deference
from inferiors.

Power is the great means to felicity, for it commands both
goods and respect.   Every man, therefore, desires power.
Hobbes puts as a "general inclination of all mankind, a
perpetual and restless desire of power after power." [11]   Desire
for power is insatiable because of the transient and invidious
nature of felicity.   Conflict between men is rooted in their
nature and unmitigated by any recognition of moral obligation.   "Justice, and injustice are none of the faculties neither
of the body, nor mind." [12]

Man's mind works in such a way as to afford him no insight into his situation and continually to lead him into
mistaken anticipations of the consequences of his actions.
Human thinking and learning processes are essentially
mechanical and blind.   According to Hobbes, "All fancies
are motions within us, relics of those made in the sense: and
those motions that immediately succeeded one another in
the sense, continue also together after sense: insomuch as the
former coming again to take place, and be predominant, the
latter followeth." [13]   For Hobbes, the prime consequence of

8 *Ibid.*, p. 50.   9 *Ibid.*, p. 111.
10 *Ibid.*   11 *Ibid.*, p. 64.
12 *Ibid.*, p. 83.
13 *Ibid.*, p. 14.   After quoting this passage, Gardner Murphy points out:
"This doctrine is basic for all associationist teaching. *Associationism* is the
doctrine that we connect things in memory, in thought, and in all mental
life, simply because they were connected in our original experience with
them; and since our first encounters with things are by means of our senses,
the associationist maintains that all the complexity of mental life is reducible
to sense impressions, the elementary components of consciousness, as connected in experience" (*Historical Introduction to Modern Psychology*, p. 26).

the operation of man's mind according to the principle of association is that he can have no "science," "the knowledge of consequences and dependence of one fact upon another." [14] Science consists of generalizations based on analysis of causes and consequences of behavior. If man cannot perform this analysis, he can have no real understanding of his situation in society.

Social processes are veiled to man. At best he can attain to "prudence," which is based on accumulation of experiences. "By how much one man has more experience of things past, than another, by so much also he is more prudent, and his expectations the seldomer fail him." [15] Reasoning consists in mechanical manipulation of one's packets of experience. "When a man *reasoneth,* he does nothing else but conceive a sum total, from *addition* of parcels; or conceive a remainder, from *subtraction* of one sum from another." [16] The mechanistic nature of man's intellectual processes dooms him to calculation without insight. In consequence his conduct is irrational, and the struggle for felicity is certain to lead to violence.

Hobbes contends that the necessary implication of his theory of human nature and dynamics is political absolutism. The function of the sovereign is to establish order and procure the safety of the people. This includes not only "a bare preservation, but also all other contentments of life, which every man by lawful industry, without danger, or hurt to the commonwealth, shall acquire to himself." [17] It is to the interest of the sovereign to promote men's material welfare, "for the good of the sovereign and people, cannot be separated." [18] Hobbes thinks the sovereign's own desire for glory and the dangers implicit in the existence of other

---

[14] Hobbes, *Leviathan,* p. 29.   [15] *Ibid.,* p. 16.
[16] *Ibid.,* p. 25.   [17] *Ibid.,* p. 219.
[18] *Ibid.,* p. 227.

sovereigns are sufficient to ensure that he will follow a policy, not of plunder, but of "Enrichissez-vous!"

He advises the sovereign to use "education, and discipline" [19] in that order of priority to control his subjects. "For the actions of men proceed from their opinions; and in the well-governing of opinions, consisteth the well-governing of men's actions, in order to their peace, and concord." [20] Censorship and indoctrination are the most effective means possessed by the sovereign to reconcile men's conflicting interests. Hobbes recommends "public instruction" [21] and asserts that "every sovereign ought to cause justice to be taught." [22] For, he says, "the common people's minds, unless they be tainted with dependence on the potent, or scribbled over with the opinions of their doctors, are like clean paper, fit to receive whatsoever by public authority shall be imprinted in them." [23] For the "potent" the prescription is the *Leviathan* itself, which ought to be required in the universities.

The *Leviathan* is not so much an attempt to show men that the consequence of irrational selfishness is mutual frustration as it is a prescription, based on the psychological doctrine of associationism, that the "laws of nature"—that is to say, justice—be stamped into men's minds through systematic indoctrination. In Hobbes's political theory man trades pride for wealth, and the job of the sovereign is to maintain the bargain intact by preaching justice and, if need be, by striking down the unjust, those who violate his law. There is a strain in the theory, however, which we may note for future reference. Hobbes assumes that man's desire for power and superiority is fixed and constant, but the principle of association implies plasticity. Man's motives may be

19 *Ibid.,* p. 460. 20 *Ibid.,* p. 116.
21 *Ibid.,* p. 219. 22 *Ibid.,* p. 223.
23 *Ibid.,* p. 221.

fixed, but they can be aimed at different goals. Hobbes argues for absolute government on the basis of the immutability of man's vainglorious striving. But when he advises the sovereign how to govern, man's capacity to be shaped by education comes to the fore. Discard Hobbes's postulate of the immutability of vaingloriousness, and what is left is a theory of human nature very much like that of the utilitarians, or, as A. D. Lindsay puts it, utilitarianism is Hobbism "with the pessimism left out." [24] Man remains a psychological, but is no longer a prideful, hedonist.

Locke's doctrine of human nature differs from Hobbes's in two essential respects. Whereas Hobbes sees man irrationally selfish, Locke sees him a fundamentally rational and social being. His objective is happiness, which he is capable of pursuing steadily and with respect for the rights of others. Conflict among men arises not so much from excessive self-love as from misunderstanding and intolerance, which have their source in illogical associations of ideas.

Locke shares with Hobbes an atomistic view of man. He enters society with his needs and purposes already formed. His nature undergoes no transformation in society of the kind Rousseau describes. To Locke, as to Hobbes, the state is essentially a "convenience" and not a necessary means to complete human development.

Man is equipped with "practical reason" by means of which he may not only appraise values correctly but also select and adhere to the line of action that promises maximum satisfaction. Locke says, "Whatever necessity determines to the pursuit of real bliss, the same necessity, with the same force, establishes suspense, deliberation, and scrutiny of each successive desire, whether the satisfaction of it does not interfere with our true happiness, and mislead us from it." [25] Human reasoning is not merely a matter

[24] Lindsay, *The Modern Democratic State*, I, 138.
[25] John Locke, *An Essay Concerning Human Understanding*, p. 187.

of association of ideas and manipulation of packets of experience, as Hobbes would have it. Reason gives man knowledge of the values which satisfy him and enables him to govern his behavior in accordance with those values.[26] Man is a rational hedonist.

Locke does not think that men invariably appraise values correctly. Their judgments as to present satisfactions are always correct. But man's "telescopic faculty" is defective; he tends to overvalue present as compared with future satisfactions. "Objects near our view are apt to be thought greater than those of a larger size that are more remote: and so it is with pleasure and pains: the present is apt to carry it, and those at a distance have the disadvantage in the comparison." [27] Men may also fail to deliberate, but they are not in constant danger of being overwhelmed by their emotions or engaging in false calculations.

Man is not only rational but also a social being. "God, having made man such a creature that, in his own judgment, it was not good for him to be alone, put him under strong obligations of necessity, convenience, and inclination, to drive him into society, as well as fitted him with understanding and language to continue and enjoy it." [28] Moreover, because man is rational he perceives that men are equal and recognizes an obligation to respect their rights—"there being nothing more evident, than that creatures of the same species and rank, promiscuously born to all the same advantages of

26 Sterling Power Lamprecht says: "Reason mixes itself with the passions in such a way as to show the relative value of the objects towards which they are directed, and thus often succeeds in transforming the passions themselves. In the end it is always the passions, alike in virtuous as in vicious conduct, which are the springs of action; but whereas in vicious conduct the passions control the man, in virtuous conduct the man may be said to control the passions" (*The Moral and Political Philosophy of John Locke*, p. 118).

27 Locke, *An Essay Concerning Human Understanding*, p. 193.

28 Locke, *Second Treatise on Civil Government*, in *Social Contract: Essays by Locke, Hume, and Rousseau*, with an Introduction by Sir Ernest Barker, p. 45.

nature, and the use of the same faculties, should also be equal one amongst another without subordination or subjection." [29]   Man's reason "is able to instruct him in that law he is to govern himself by, and make him known how far he is left to the freedom of his own will." [30]   Thus man is not only a rational hedonist but also social and moral.   His reason dictates just behavior.   He has a conscience.

Locke qualifies his view of the social nature of man somewhat.   Although men understand they ought to treat one another justly, they do not always do so.   In his analysis of the "state of nature," Locke holds that "were it not for the corruption and viciousness of degenerate men, there would be no need of any other, no necessity that men should separate from this great and natural community, and associate into less combinations." [31]   "Degenerate men" are not the only ones whose actions depart from the standard of justice.   All men are to some extent actuated by self-love, which introduces an element of bias into their behavior and judgment.   "Though the law of nature be plain and intelligible to all rational creatures, yet men, being biased by their interest, as well as ignorant for want of study of it, are not apt to allow of it as a law binding to them in the application of it to their particular cases." [32]   Psychological hedonism and ignorance make existence in the "state of nature" uncertain and dangerous.   Their self-preference is the basic reason why men leave the "state of nature" for civil society.   "The inconveniences that they are therein exposed to by the irregular and uncertain exercise of the power every man has of punishing the transgressions of others,

29 *Ibid.,* p. 4.   30 *Ibid.,* p. 36.
31 *Ibid.,* pp. 74-75.
32 *Ibid.,* p. 73.   J. W. Gough says: "The law of nature is not innate; what is knowable by the light of nature is the kind of truth at which a man may arrive, by himself and without extraneous help, through the right use of the faculties with which he was endowed by nature" (*John Locke's Political Philosophy: Eight Studies,* p. 14).

make them take sanctuary under the established laws of government, and therein seek the preservation of their property." [33] Thus Locke does not regard man as entirely social and just. But these qualifications do not vitiate his fundamental conclusion as to the sociability of man's nature. Willmoore Kendall says that "the evidence is not conclusive, but it does suggest that Locke would have subscribed to the proposition that a 'safe' majority of men (thus the 'average' man) are rational and just." [34] Some men are more rational than others, but this difference is the result of their ownership of property and not innate.[35]

There is another reason besides man's self-interestedness and ignorance why he is liable to behave in an irrational or unjust manner. His intellectual processes depend largely on the principle of association. Establishment of illogical associations of ideas produces unreasonable behavior. "Some such wrong and unnatural combination of ideas will be found to establish the irreconcilable opposition between different sects of philosophy and religion."[36] Illogical association "has such an influence, and is of so great force, to set us awry in our actions, as well moral as natural, passions, reasonings, and notions themselves, that perhaps there is not any one thing that deserves more to be looked after." [37] The purpose of education must be to establish valid associations.

It would appear that no two theories of man could be more different from one another than those held by Hobbes and Locke. Hobbes regards man as an irrational, prideful and

[33] Locke, *Second Treatise on Civil Government,* in *Social Contract: Essays by Locke, Hume, and Rousseau,* p. 74.

[34] Kendall, *John Locke and the Doctrine of Majority Rule,* p. 134.

[35] C. B. Macpherson says, "With Locke the difference in rationality was not inherent in men; it was socially acquired by virtue of different economic positions" ("The Social Bearing of Locke's Political Theory," *The Western Political Quarterly,* VII [March, 1954], 16).

[36] Locke, *An Essay Concerning Human Understanding,* p. 319.

[37] *Ibid.,* p. 317.

antisocial creature.   Locke sees him fundamentally rational
and social, although self-interested and biased.   These differences, however, conceal an even more profound similarity.
Neither Hobbes nor Locke envisages men undergoing transformation of their nature in society as does Rousseau.   They
agree on the nature of the functional relationship between
man's psychological processes and his environment.   This
acts on him only according to the principle of association.
It is this agreement between their theories of human nature
which above all distinguishes them from Rousseau's conception of man.

Against Hobbes, Rousseau contends that man is not innately selfish and vain; against Locke, he contends that man
is not innately sociable and moral.   Neither theory deals
with necessary expressions of human tendencies in society.
Man may be, according to Rousseau, either prideful or social
and moral depending on the nature of his education and
environment.   In other words, Hobbes and Locke regard
as necessary what Rousseau thinks are contingent expressions
of man's nature.

From the viewpoint of Hobbes and Locke, the effect of his
environment on man may be described in terms of the
doctrine of associationism.   For Hobbes especially this
doctrine provides a sufficient explanation of man's thinking
and learning processes.   It also accounts for relations between
intellectual and motivational processes.   Rousseau, however,
thinks human development can be a natural unfolding of
autonomous tendencies in an appropriate environment.
Man's attitudes, emotions, and motives depend on the extent
to which his capacity for rational insight is developed.   This
dependence is seen as necessary and lawful.   Given understanding of himself and his relations to others, man necessarily acquires a conscience which motivates him to behave
in a just manner.   Without this understanding, he is a
conscienceless, prideful creature striving to outdo his fellows.

Rousseau is, of course, fully aware of the principle of association, and we have seen his use of it. But he does not think it the only principle which underlies psychological processes.

Hobbes's and Locke's theories of human nature and dynamics differ from Rousseau's on the points of functional relations between psychological processes and between these and man's environment. For Rousseau, emotional and motivational processes depend on intellectual processes, and these in turn depend on the kind of environment in which man has been brought to maturity. For Hobbes and Locke, environment does not affect the expression of innate tendencies. Man is to one inherently selfish and prideful, to the other, inherently social and moral. But environment does affect what man learns, it is the source of his associations. For Rousseau, environment does affect the expression of innate tendencies, it determines whether man will be a prideful or a conscientious being. Learning need not be a process of conditioning based on the principle of association. It may be a process of transformation based on respect for man's autonomous tendencies.

What Rousseau does in his theory of human nature and dynamics is in effect to synthesize the views of Hobbes and Locke. He recognizes the existence in man of both egoistic and moral potentialities, and argues that release of these potentialities depends on the nature of man's environment. But if this is the case, then man's relation to his environment cannot be described in terms of the doctrine of associationism alone. It can be explained only by a principle of transformation. But it is not an arbitrary transformation that man undergoes in society. For it depends on the nature of his potentialities. Man develops in, rather than is moulded by, society. Here is the novelty in Rousseau's view of human nature.

9

HIS DIFFERENCES FROM CLASSICAL LIBERALISM

T HE MAIN CURRENTS of classical liberal democratic theory flow around rather than through Rousseau. Although he shares many of the values and aspirations of classical liberalism, his ideas about man and the state differ from its pattern of thought in significant ways. The purpose of this chapter is to reveal the nature of these differences, especially with reference to English utilitarianism from which modern liberalism has mainly evolved.

The outstanding common characteristic of the theories of human nature held by Hobbes and Locke is their environmentalism. The implication of the doctrine of associationism is that man may be shaped almost at will by manipulation of his environment. In the face of this possibility, it becomes relatively unimportant whether man is also regarded as predominantly an egoistic or a social being. If he is plastic, there is ground for optimism about his social future. Progress is not, of course, a necessary implication of human plasticity. Indeed, retrogression is equally possible. But the classical liberals chose to think progress inevitable. By changing his environment, they hoped to shape man in the image of their moral ideals.

In France during the eighteenth century the influence of Locke was dominant. According to Charles Frankel, it was Locke who gave the Enlightenment reason to believe that "man could control his destiny, that the mind could be made the creature of a planned environment in which it would conform with the infallible rules of morality. His philosophy was the original source of the optimistic determinism of the French Revolution." [1] Above all, man's plasticity meant to French liberals that he was capable of moral improvement. J. B. Bury points out that "this doctrine of the possibility of infinitely moulding the characters of men by laws and institutions . . . laid a foundation on which the theory of the perfectibility of humanity could be raised." [2] The optimism of the Enlightenment was heightened by the belief that the development of social institutions was in actuality beneficent. Man was not only susceptible to environmental influence but was in fact being moulded toward perfection. Cassirer says, "Diderot and the Encyclopaedists are convinced that one can entrust himself to the progress of culture because such progress, simply by virtue of its immanent tendency and law, will of itself bring about a better form of the social order." [3] With reference to Rousseau and Diderot, Cassirer asserts that "the decisive contrast between the two men" lies in the fact that Diderot accepts and Rousseau rejects the idea of an "immanent tendency and law" of progress. [4]

As we have seen, Rousseau does not think in terms of an automatic correspondence between the nature of man's potentialities and his social environment. For Rousseau, man has authentic needs which may or may not be met by his society. Society must be organized in accordance with these human requirements, and there is no guarantee that such organization will come about without man's intervention in

[1] Frankel, *The Faith of Reason: The Idea of Progress in the French Enlightenment,* p. 43.

[2] Bury, *The Idea of Progress,* p. 167.

[3] Ernst Cassirer, *The Philosophy of the Enlightenment,* trans. Fritz C. A. Koelln and James P. Pettegrove, p. 268.

[4] *Ibid.*

the historical process, deliberate intervention based on an understanding of man's autonomous tendencies.[5] Progress is possible, but it must be the achievement of reason, not the result of history. As Frankel says:

The problem for Rousseau was to establish those conditions that would provide outlets for the naturally good instincts of the "natural" man. . . . Rousseau was an opponent of the continuing progress of the dominant institutions of the *ancien régime* because that progress was really decadence, and because he regarded himself as an apostle of human progress, of the perfectibility of the natural man, when it is rightly understood.[6]

Rousseau thinks progress possible, not actual. This outlook is quite different from that produced by the combination of Locke's psychological theory and the assumption that there exists an automatic tendency toward harmony between man and his environment.

It is not that the philosophers of the Enlightenment believed in reason and Rousseau did not. He was as concerned as any to develop man's capacity to reason. But Rousseau was no rationalist in the sense of believing in the existence of an automatic harmonizing of men's interests. His rationalism took the form of the belief that human interests could be harmonious. "If the clashing of particular interests made the establishment of societies necessary, the agreement of these very interests made it possible." [7] Harmonization of interests, as Rousseau conceives it, requires much more than diffusion of knowledge, as the *philosophes* were wont to be-

[5] According to Bernard Groethuysen, "There exists between Rousseau and the *philosophes* of his time an opposition of principle in the way of viewing human life and determining its ends. For the *philosophes* of the eighteenth century, human values are always in accord with historical and social development. One cannot direct individuals without knowing the ends presented by the society in which they live" (*Jean-Jacques Rousseau*, p. 49). Author's translation.

[6] Charles Frankel, *The Faith of Reason*, p. 80.

[7] Rousseau, *The Social Contract*, Book ii, ch. 1.

lieve. It is not the inevitable outcome of historical development. The natural drift of society is toward prideful
materialism, toward more severe differences of interest.
Harmony and progress require nothing less than the recast-
ing of social and political institutions in accordance with the
dynamics of human nature. Perfectibility is not immanent
in history but rather a possibility, the realization of which
depends on rational insight and moral effort.

Rousseau also stands outside the pattern of classical liberal
democratic thought in so far as it contains a belief in the
existence of self-evident and specific natural rights which
man inherits from a "state of nature." He does not postulate
the existence of natural rights, as we have pointed out, except in the sense of a generalized right of man to the development of his potentialities. This conception of natural right
links Rousseau to the thought of some modern liberals,[8] but
it just as surely separates him from classical liberalism.

In England, classical liberalism took the form of utilitarianism. Here the influence of Hobbes, rather than of Locke,
was dominant. The utilitarians, Jeremy Bentham and James
Mill, think man is as egoistic a creature as does Hobbes.
But in their psychology Hobbes's postulate of the immutability of vainglorious striving is displaced by environmentalism. Man may be egoistic, but because the operation
of his mind is governed by the principle of association, he
may be made social—that is to say, taught to identify his
interest with the general interest. He may be a psychological, but he need not be a prideful, hedonist. Utilitarian
conduct, if not intent, can be built into his nature.

Moreover, the utilitarians think that the selfish interests of
men tend to harmonize. Pennock says, "Faith in the rational
order of the universe persisted in the form of the belief that
the combination of individual, self-seeking interests would

---

8 See J. Roland Pennock, *Liberal Democracy: Its Merits and Prospects*,
pp. 101ff.

produce a harmonious pattern of social well being." [9] Thus the psychology of Hobbes was transformed into the basis for a social philosophy no less optimistic than that of the Enlightenment.

According to the utilitarians' theory of human nature and dynamics, man is a psychological hedonist whose psychological processes are governed by the principle of association.[10] Bentham emphasizes the hedonistic aspect of this view of man, while James Mill, in his *Analysis of the Phenomena of the Human Mind* [11] concentrates on explaining mental operations in terms of the doctrine of associationism.

Bentham thinks man's behavior is, and ought to be, governed by the "principle of utility." "Nature has placed mankind under the governance of two sovereign masters, *pain* and *pleasure*. It is for them alone to point out what we ought to do, as well as to determine what we shall do. On the one hand the standard of right and wrong, on the other the chain of causes and effects, are fastened to their throne." [12] The "principle of utility" is an amalgam of a normative and a positive proposition about man's nature, and for Bentham it serves simultaneously as a standard of morals and legislation and as an analysis of man's motivational processes. "By the principle of utility is meant that principle which approves or disapproves of every action whatsoever, according to the tendency which it appears to

9 *Ibid.*, p. 18.

10 Harry K. Girvetz says: "Whatever the practical considerations which inspired psychological hedonism, its theoretical source is to be found in the associational psychology which, beginning with Hobbes, almost completely dominated English and French thought for two centuries. Because a satisfied desire is *associated* with or accompanied by pleasure, it was assumed that pleasure is the object or motive of all desire" (*From Wealth to Welfare: The Evolution of Liberalism*, p. 13).

11 James Mill, *Analysis of the Phenomena of the Human Mind*, 2 vols.

12 Jeremy Bentham, *An Introduction to the Principles of Morals and Legislation*, in *A Fragment on Government and An Introduction to the Principles of Morals and Legislation*, ed. by Wilfrid Harrison, p. 125.

have to augment or diminish the happiness of the party whose interest is in question." [13]   Men tend to act on the basis of this principle, and if they do not so act, then they evaluate their actions in terms of it.   "By the natural constitution of the human frame, on most occasions of their lives men in general embrace this principle, without thinking of it: if not for the ordering of their own actions, yet for the trying of their own actions, as well as those of other men." [14]   This is to say that men are egoists, but are, or ought to be, enlightened egoists.   Some motives are more likely than others to result in behavior in conformity with the principle of utility.   "For the dictates of utility are neither more nor less than the dictates of the most extensive and enlightened (that is *well-advised*) benevolence." [15]   It is no narrow egoistic hedonism that Bentham advocates but rather a rational hedonism which takes into account the consequences of one's actions as they return upon one's self.

For Bentham, government is essentially a device for increasing the rationality of man's conduct.

Private ethics teaches how each man may dispose himself to pursue the course most conducive to his own happiness, by means of such motives as offer of themselves: the art of legislation . . . teaches how a multitude of men, composing a community, may be disposed to pursue that course which upon the whole is the most conducive to the happiness of the whole community, by means of motives to be applied by the legislator.[16]

In other words, the individual applies the principle of utility to his own behavior, and the legislator applies it to the behavior of all individuals in society.   It is the government that ensures that the effort of each to maximize his own happiness is consistent with the like efforts of all the others.

James Mill builds upon Bentham's psychological and moral theories an argument for democracy.   From an

13 *Ibid.*, p. 126.   14 *Ibid.*, p. 128.
15 *Ibid.*, p. 236.   16 *Ibid.*, p. 423.

analytical standpoint, there are two problems for which utilitarians must find solutions. First, there must be assurance that men will act on the basis of the principle of utility, and secondly, a way must be found to ensure that the government will apply it. James Mill undertakes to solve both these problems. The solution to the first is education and to the second, democracy.

According to Mill, wealth, power, and dignity are the principal means by which men may obtain pleasure, because they make possible command of the services of others. These means may also be used for the purpose of invidious display. He says:

It is to be observed, that Wealth, Power, and Dignity, derive a great portion of their efficacy, from their comparative amount; that is, from their being possessed in greater quantity than most other people possess them. In contemplating them with the satisfaction with which powerful causes of pleasure are contemplated, we seldom fail to include the comparison. And the state of consciousness, formed by the contemplation and comparison taken together, is called Pride.[17]

Pride is a dangerous attitude in Mill's view, for it tends to divert men from the principle of utility. Under its influence they behave irrationally; they mistake means for ends. He says, "Wealth, Power, and Dignity, afford perhaps the most remarkable of all examples of that extraordinary case of association, where the means to an end, means valuable to us solely on account of their end, not only engross more of our affection than the end itself, but actually supplant it in our affections." [18]   Mill is eloquent in recital of the dismal effects of this "extraordinary case of association":

How few men seem to be at all concerned about their fellow-creatures? How completely are the lives of most men absorbed, in the pursuits of wealth, and ambition! With how many does

17 James Mill, *Analysis of the Phenomena of the Human Mind,* II, 213.
18 *Ibid.,* p. 215.

the love of Family, of Friend, of Country, of Mankind, appear completely impotent, when opposed to their love of Wealth, or of Power! This is an effect of misguided association, and which requires the greatest attention in Education, and morals.[19]

That perpetual and restless inclination of all mankind, of which Hobbes had spoken, becomes the "effect of misguided association."

The proper association, according to Mill, is that between the idea of one's own pleasures and the idea of those of other people. "There is nothing which more instantly associates with itself the ideas of our own Pleasures, and Pains, than the idea of the Pleasures and Pains of another of our Fellow-creatures." [20] But this association requires to be strengthened by education if it is to become an effective motive to action. Then men will behave in accordance with the principle of utility, insensitive to the diversions of pridefulness. "That man may be justly said to have the greatest command over his ideas, whose associations with the grand sources of felicity are the most numerous and strong. When the grand sources of felicity are formed into the leading and governing ideas, each in its due and relative strength, Education has then performed its most perfect work; and thus the individual becomes, to the greatest degree, the source of utility to others, and of happiness to himself." [21] James Mill intends by means of "Education" to stamp into men's minds the right associations and thereby to ensure that they pursue their satisfaction in a rational manner. Utilitarian behavior is to be built into man. Not understanding, but rather automatic responsiveness in accordance with the principle of utility is the goal of his education.

To ensure that the government will apply the principle of utility, Mill argues that it must be democratic. The prime political implication of the Benthamistic view of human

19 *Ibid.*   20 *Ibid.*, pp. 216-17.
21 *Ibid.*, p. 378.

nature is thought to be democracy. How does it come about, asks Halévy, that the "philosophy of Hobbes leads to conclusions which contradict the constitutional theories of Hobbes himself." [22]   According to Halévy, Bentham and Mill see that the "majority are the strongest, and moreover . . . the will of the greatest number is the surest protector of the interest of the greatest number." [23]   John Plamenatz says, "They happened to be more afraid of misgovernment than anarchy." [24]   Mill was afraid of misgovernment because of man's desire for power.

In his *Essay on Government*, called by Ernest Barker the "classical statement of the political theory of the Benthamites," [25] Mill says:

That one human being will desire to render the person and property of another subservient to his pleasures, notwithstanding the pain or loss of pleasure which it may occasion to that other individual, is the foundation of Government. The desire of the object implies the desire of the power necessary to accomplish the object. The desire, therefore, of that power which is necessary to render the persons and properties of human beings subservient to our pleasures, is a grand governing law of human nature.[26]

On this view of human nature there is positive danger in a despotic, Hobbesian government. All members of the government will desire to use the citizens and their property for gratification of their desires, and by the relentless logic of their associationistic minds will be led to establish a regime of extreme brutality. Mill claims, "The very principle of human nature upon which the necessity of Government is founded . . . leads on, by infallible sequence, where power over a community is attained, and nothing

[22] Elie Halévy, *The Growth of Philosophic Radicalism,* trans. Mary Morris, p. 431.
[23] *Ibid.*
[24] Plamenatz, *The English Utilitarians,* p. 16.
[25] Barker, "Introduction," in James Mill, *An Essay on Government,* p. xiv.
[26] James Mill, *An Essay on Government,* p. 17.

checks, not only to that degree of plunder which leaves the members . . . the bare means of subsistence, but to that degree of cruelty which is necessary to keep in existence the most intense terror." [27]   This is to disregard Hobbes's contention that competition among sovereigns serves as a check on each.   But if Mill's government is not prideful, it is logical to assume that its members will be less interested in glory than in plunder.

From the "grand governing law of human nature," Mill argues that the government must not only be democratic but must also be based on the principle of "lessening of duration" of its term of office.   He says, "The smaller the period of time during which any man retains his capacity of Representative, as compared with the time in which he is simply a member of the community, the more difficult it will be to compensate the sacrifice of the interests of the longer period, by the profits of misgovernment during the shorter." [28] Democracy is to the Benthamites a sort of mutual protection system.   The danger to all of the governors' acting for their selfish interests is to be neutralized by forcing them to identify their interests with those of the community.   Democracy makes it to their interest to apply the principle of utility in legislation.

It is apparent that Rousseau's ideas about man and the state, except where these are based on the doctrine of associationism, differ substantially from the utilitarian pattern of thought.   In comparison with his view of human nature, the utilitarian psychology represents a tremendous simplification. Man is governed by a single motive, that of maximizing his pleasures; and his psychological processes function according to a single principle, that of association.   Benthamite man is a thoroughgoing egoist; his relationship to his social environment is essentially exploitative.   Furthermore, he does not depend on his environment for the development of his

[27] *Ibid.,* p. 23.   [28] *Ibid.,* p. 38.

capacities, and he undergoes no transformation in society of the kind Rousseau describes. He may be moulded by education and controlled by law, and so seem a more rational creature than Rousseau's man. But even this rationality is purchased, so to speak, at the price of limited understanding. For his rationality, which consists in a strong tendency to behave in accordance with his long run interests, is the product of the establishment of associations between the goal of happiness and the means that will obtain it.[29]

Education does not mean to the utilitarians, as it does to the Rousseau of *Émile,* the development of man's capacity for insight into himself and social processes. Rather it means the deliberate indoctrination of man in accordance with what appear to be the necessities of his environment. It is comparable to Rousseau's proposal for patriotic education. Certainty of response rather than adaptability and understanding is its aim. As Machiavelli pointed out, men who do not understand their environment cannot hope to conquer "fortune,"—that is to say, to change appropriately with changes in that environment.[30] In comparison with the utilitarian conception of reason, Rousseau's account of

[29] Note Gunnar Myrdal's observation: "Liberalism was a rationalistic philosophy. Its contribution to the science of psychology was shallow hedonism and the theory of intellectual associations. In economics its rationalistic principles were elaborated in the marginal theory of value and in the utilitarian deduction of general welfare out of the enlightened self-interest of the individual. But when rational hedonism had actually begun to spread and people really started to think and act a little more like the liberal theory's 'economic man,' the bottom fell out of liberal economic society.

"The explanation of this paradox is that, contrary to all the theorizing about man of this intellectualistic and rationalistic liberal philosophy, its basic assumptions—atomism and a static frame of society and static social attitudes—implied the prevalence in society of human beings who were the very opposite to the rationalistic 'economic man' of its theory. They had to be traditionalistic, strongly inhibited by existing taboos, never questioning, non-experimental, non-reflecting conventionalists" ("The Trend towards Economic Planning," *The Manchester School of Economic and Social Studies,* XIX [Jan., 1951], 11).

[30] Machiavelli, *The Prince,* ch. 25.

human intelligence may be described as rationalistic. Indeed, Rousseau emerges from the comparison a devotee of human rationality. He may not think man so likely to behave in accordance with his self-interest as do the utilitarians. But his conception of reason and its relation to other psychological processes makes it much more central to man's nature than does theirs.

According to the utilitarians, the fact of society does not cause new needs to arise in man. He has but a single and invariant motive, that of seeking his own pleasure. This is his only autonomous tendency. Except for the motive of pleasure, the human character is plastic and ready to be shaped according to the wishes of the educator. There is no capacity in man to respond to the needs of others which may, in the proper environment, develop into a sense of justice and obligation. Indeed, man does not develop at all according to this conception of human nature, other than in the sense of becoming a more enlightened and persistent hedonist.

It is clear, then, that Rousseau's account of human nature and dynamics is more complex than that of Bentham and James Mill. The crucial difference lies in the way they view the relation between man and society. For Rousseau, man depends on society for what he is, in the sense that only in society may his potentialities be realized or violated. For Bentham and Mill, man depends on society for his satisfactions, which are obtained through utilization of his fellows—either wisely or foolishly, depending on the associations which form the contents of his mind.[31] In Rousseau's view, society is essential to the very existence of man in that he is not truly human outside a social environment. From the utilitarian standpoint, society is merely instrumental to man.

[31] Frank H. Knight says, "The Economic man neither competes nor higgles —nor does he co-operate, psychologically speaking; he treats other human beings as if they were slot machines" ("Ethics and Economic Reform," in *Freedom and Reform: Essays in Economics and Social Philosophy*, p. 66).

It is not necessary for the release of human personality, but rather for the satisfaction of innate purpose, namely, pleasure.

The utilitarians reach the same conclusion that Rousseau does on the desirable form of government, democracy. But this similarity in their political theories conceals more than it reveals. The significance of political institutions is quite differently understood by Rousseau and the utilitarians. For them, the state is essentially a device for controlling man so as to bring his conduct into closer conformity with the principle of utility; it rationalizes his behavior. Rousseau sees the state as essential to the right development of man, and law as the guarantee of moral action. They think democracy is the only way to control man's selfishness. For him, it is the only form of government that does not place men in a position of "personal dependence." It is essential, therefore, to the release of moral potentialities, not merely to the neutralization of egoistic biases. Only democracy is consistent with his ideals of moral autonomy and responsibility.

If we consider now the modifications of the classical liberal democratic pattern of thought made by John Stuart Mill, we shall see that these bring it into closer relationship with Rousseau's ideas. John Stuart Mill's view of human nature is distinguished from that held by his father and by Bentham by an emphasis on man's social instinct taken in the sense of a need for social unity. Because he also retains the Benthamite view of man's egoistic tendencies, his theory of human nature presents man as an ambivalent, almost contradictory creature. Furthermore, John Stuart Mill envisages man as far more dependent than do the Benthamites upon his social and political environment for development of his capacities. Thus on the score of both ambivalence and social dependence his conception of man is closer to Rousseau's than is that of the Benthamites. It will not be surprising, therefore, to find that the political theories of

John Stuart Mill and Rousseau exhibit some striking similarities.

According to Mill, human nature includes a "powerful natural sentiment"—namely, the "desire to be in unity with our fellow creatures." [32] He says, "Already a person in whom the social feeling is at all developed, cannot bring himself to think of the rest of his fellow-creatures as struggling rivals with him for the means of happiness, whom he must desire to see defeated in their object that he may succeed in his." [33] This is to say that man is a rather more social being than the Benthamites had thought. But existence of "the social feeling" does not mean that man is not also self-interested and desirous of power. Mill says, "Human beings are only secure from evil at the hands of others in proportion as they have the power of being, and are, self-*protecting*." [34] Moreover, man's nature is not plastic in the way the Benthamites believed it to be. "Human nature is not a machine to be built after a model, and set to do exactly the work prescribed for it, but a tree, which requires to grow and develop itself on all sides, according to the tendency of the inward forces which make it a living thing." [35] Mill does not abandon associationism entirely, but he sees man as having autonomous tendencies which must be taken into account in designing his social environment.

On the basis of this view of human nature, Mill asserts that political institutions have a much more significant contribution to make to human development than the Benthamites believed possible. This contribution is made especially through the "spirit" of political institutions, which Mill describes as "that portion of their influence which is least regarded by common, and especially by English, thinkers; though the institutions of every country, not under

32 John Stuart Mill, *Utilitarianism*, p. 194.
33 *Ibid.*, p. 196.
34 John Stuart Mill, *Considerations on Representative Government*, p. 142.
35 John Stuart Mill, *On Liberty*, p. 52.

great positive oppression, produce more effect by their spirit than by any of their direct provisions, since by it they shape the national character." [36]   Mill speaks of government as a "great influence acting on the human mind" [37] and as an "agency of national education." [38]

Political institutions may promote development of social feeling in men.   Through participation in government by serving on juries, by holding posts in local administration, and by voting, social interest is stimulated.   "It is not sufficiently considered how little there is in most men's ordinary life to give any largeness either to their conceptions or to their sentiments. . . .   Giving him something to do for the public, supplies, in a measure, all these deficiencies." [39] Not only participation in the work of government but also discussion of political issues, Mill sees as making a contribution to the development of man's social nature.   "It is from political discussion, and collective political action, that one whose daily occupations concentrate his interests in a small circle round himself, learns to feel for and with his fellow-citizens, and becomes consciously a member of a great community." [40]   Mill expects political activity to promote development of man's capacity for social sentiment.   He does not rely upon the establishment of proper associations and legal sanctions to obtain social behavior, as did the Benthamites.   His approach is rather to provide men with activities that call forth their social emotions and attitudes.

Because he doubts that man is so rational a creature as the Benthamites had supposed,[41] Mill's conception of the in-

---

36 John Stuart Mill, *Representative Government*, p. 221.
37 *Ibid.*, p. 129.   38 *Ibid.*, p. 130.
39 *Ibid.*, pp. 149-50.   40 *Ibid.*, p. 211.
41 Of the "labouring classes," John Stuart Mill says: "It is not what their interest is, but what they suppose it to be, that is the important consideration with respect to their conduct: and it is quite conclusive against any theory of government that it assumes the numerical majority to do habitually what is never done, nor expected to be done, save in very exceptional cases, by any other depositaries of power—namely, to direct their conduct

stitutions that will produce just and responsible government is different from theirs. His father had thought in terms of highly responsive government, not only because he feared misgovernment, but also because he thought men likely to know what policies were in their real interest. At least they could be expected to identify those who knew and would pursue such policies. For John Stuart Mill, this is grossly to oversimplify the process of government. Indeed, from Mill's standpoint, his father dangerously misconceives the nature of both political and social processes. John Stuart Mill refers to that "antagonism of influences which is the only real security for continued progress." [42] Much more than merely responsive government is required to maintain this "antagonism of influences."

Mill gives his endorsement to the scheme of proportional representation because he sees in it a way to ensure the deliberation on policy that he deems so important. Because of the "danger of class legislation; of government intended for . . . the immediate benefit of the dominant class, to the lasting detriment of the whole," Mill thinks that in the construction of a representative system "the desirable object would be that no class, and no combination of classes likely to combine, should be able to exercise a preponderant influence in the government." [43] Proportional representation not only prevents class domination of the legislature, but also would help to ensure that justice prevails there.

The reason why, in any tolerably constituted society, justice and the general interest mostly in the end carry their point, is that

---

by their real ultimate interest, in opposition to their immediate and apparent interest" (*Representative Government*, p. 183). James Mill had relied on an association in the people's mind between wealth and power with dignity on the one hand, and dignity with a benevolent disposition on the other, in his argument that the people would vote for those who understood their interests, that is, the middle class. See *An Essay on Government*, pp. 48-49, 72.

[42] John Stuart Mill, *Representative Government*, p. 134.

[43] *Ibid.*, p. 187.

the separate and selfish interests of mankind are almost always divided; some are interested in what is wrong, but some, also, have their private interest on the side of what is right: and those who are governed by higher considerations, though too few and weak to prevail against the whole of the others, usually after sufficient discussion and agitation become strong enough to turn the balance in favour of the body of private interests which is on the same side with them.[44]

A legislature based on proportional representation is seen by Mill as the one in which this process of cancelling out of selfish interests is most likely to take place, and thus permit what Rousseau calls the general will to be expressed.

From Rousseau's standpoint, it may be said that Mill envisages the formation of two general wills: one in society, based on the "antagonism of influences"; and the other within the legislature, based on its reflection of the differing interests in society. Rousseau rejected representative government partly because he thought personal and group biases of the representative would prevent expression of the general will. Mill's view of how a representative body may be organized so as to tend to reach just decisions would appear to go far towards meeting Rousseau's objection. We do not mean to imply, of course, that Mill deliberately set about to solve a problem which confronted Rousseau. But from an analytical standpoint, what Mill does is to seek to solve the problem of representation of the general will through its duplication in the legislature.

Mill's idea of the educational influence of the "spirit" of political institutions is quite in line with Rousseau's thought on how government affects human development. Both see man as much more dependent on his social environment for what he is than did the Benthamites. Mill's conception of social dependence is not, however, so far-reaching as Rousseau's. Mill looks at social feeling as a distinct and

44 *Ibid.*, p. 188.

definite impulse planted in man's nature. Political participation and discussion are sufficient to call it forth. Rousseau thinks that social sentiment arises somewhat less spontaneously. At least, to be sufficiently intense for political stability it must be manufactured. No doubt he does think political participation essential to generate group feeling. But it is precisely at this point in his political theory that Rousseau shifts from reliance on the principle of transformation to use of the principle of association.

An important consequence flows from this theoretical difference between Mill and Rousseau on the relationship of man to his social environment. Mill views economic interests and materialism generally as posing much less serious a threat to social unity than does Rousseau. There is something almost Hobbesian in Mill's statement: "That the energies of mankind should be kept in employment by the struggle for riches, as they were formerly by the struggle of war until the better minds succeed in educating the others into better things, is undoubtedly more desirable than that they should rust and stagnate." [45] According to Mill's psychological theory, pursuit of economic interests may even tend to strengthen man's social feeling. "The person bestirring himself with hopeful prospects to improve his circumstances is the one who feels good-will towards others engaged in, or who have succeeded in, the same pursuit." [46] He takes a much more sanguine view of the social and political consequences of economic activity than does Rousseau. The latter thinks economic interests are inherently divisive, and seeks to sublimate them in the emotional fire of patriotism. Mill's attitude is more like that of the Benthamites, who thought in terms of an almost automatic harmonization of selfish interests within the rules laid

[45] John Stuart Mill, *Principles of Political Economy, with Some of Their Applications to Social Philosophy,* p. 749.
[46] John Stuart Mill, *Representative Government,* p. 146.

down by government.[47]   It is this belief, which, perhaps more than any other, accounts for the indifference shown by all of the utilitarians to deliberate cultivation of group feeling.   John Stuart Mill is not so indifferent as the others. But intensification of social sentiment is not a matter of paramount importance to him, as it became to Rousseau. It should be kept in mind, of course, that Mill had seen, as Rousseau had not, the spontaneous growth of nationalistic sentiment during the nineteenth century.

If we attempt to summarize the results of our comparison of Rousseau's ideas about man and the state with the classical pattern of liberal democratic thought, we see that the differences between them stem from Rousseau's conception of men's radical psychological and moral interdependence.   In society men depend on one another for what they are.   For Rousseau, this does not mean that man is plastic only in the sense that his goals and attitudes may be shaped by education and indoctrination.   He is that to the extent his psychological processes are governed by the principle of association. But his nature is also capable of transformation in a social environment, a transformation based ultimately on rational insight into his own nature and society.   It is this idea that is absent from the classical liberals' thought about human nature.   Because Rousseau views man in this way, political institutions have a significance for him that they do not for Bentham and James Mill.   Political institutions are not merely means by which men may more effectively pursue their purposes consistently with an ethical principle they cannot follow for its own sake.   Rather these institutions are

[47] Note Lionel Robbins statement: "Bentham would have rejected, as inherently self-contradictory, any idea of a distinction between an artificial harmony created by law and a spontaneous harmony created by economic behavior.   In so far as there was harmony at all, the harmony created by law was the harmony arising from behavior within the framework of the law. There was no dualism in this respect, the conception was essentially one and indivisible" (*The Theory of Economic Policy in English Classical Political Economy*, p. 192).

crucial to the determination of the purposes men will have. Whether men are egoistically or productively oriented depends on the way in which their society is politically organized.

John Stuart Mill's conception of the "spirit" of political institutions derives from his conception of man's social dependence and links his thought to Rousseau's. But he makes social emotion more central to man's nature than does Rousseau, and so they diverge on the question of the need for creating group feeling. Perhaps the most striking similarity in the political theory of Mill and Rousseau is their belief in the need for an "antagonism of influences" to ensure that the general will be expressed and justice prevail. But here again they diverge on the way to bring this antagonism to bear in legislation. Rousseau will not consider representative government because he thinks it fatal to social spirit, whereas Mill thinks it the only form of democratic government possible in the large society.

To the extent that the classical liberals entertain the idea of an automatic harmonizing of men's interests, they diverge from Rousseau's way of thinking. He is sceptical of any form of automatic harmony, whether it be immanent in the historical process or the outcome of rational economic activity and striving. Rousseau does think there can be social harmony. But men must create it for themselves by establishing institutions that call forth their moral potentialities and ensure reliable political deliberation.

Chapter

10

GENERAL WILL AND THE DELIBERATIVE STATE

THE DISTINCTIVE characteristic of modern liberalism is that it envisages creation of social harmony through an elaborate process of discussion. Central to modern liberal doctrine is the theory of the deliberative state. One of its leading exponents, A. D. Lindsay, says, "All this process of discussion is, however complicated and arranged for, a natural process —grounded in the facts of human nature." [1] If this is the case, the modern liberal view of man must be rather different from that expounded by the Benthamites. To compare Rousseau's theory of the general will with the theory of the deliberative state, we need first to see just how and why modern liberalism differs from the classical variety. It should be kept in mind, of course, that the distinction between classical and modern liberalism is somewhat arbitrary from a historical standpoint. There is no sharp break in the evolution of liberal doctrine. John Stuart Mill has one foot in each camp. He looks backward towards Benthamism when he says, "Education and opinion, which have so vast a power over human character, should so use that power as to establish in the mind of every individual an indissoluble association between his own happiness and the good of the whole." [2] He looks forward to modern liberalism when he

1 Lindsay, *The Essentials of Democracy,* p. 41.
2 John Stuart Mill, *Utilitarianism,* p. 179.

affirms, "It really is of importance, not only what men do, but also what manner of men they are that do it." [3] Our central concern, however, is not with the evolution of liberal doctrine, but rather with differences between its classical and modern versions. Attention is given to the way in which liberal doctrine evolved only for the purpose of elucidating these differences.

Modern liberalism in the sense of the theory of the deliberative state is the outcome of revolt against two leading features of the classical liberal democratic pattern of thought. Modern liberalism rejects the associationistic psychology that is integral to classical liberalism. And the notion that social processes, especially economic processes, may be blind and, therefore, require control, replaces the classical assumption of a more or less self-regulating society. The revolt took place in stages, however. The classical pattern of thought was not discarded all at once, and never completely. It will be helpful, therefore, to examine the way in which modern liberalism evolved from classical liberalism. No doubt Rousseau has had great influence on modern liberal thinking, but again the nature of this influence is not our concern. This is analytical not historical. The question we ask is: Why has modern liberalism come to regard discussion as the essence of democratic political processes?

A change in liberal thinking about man and the state may be said to have begun in the work of T. H. Green. He sees man much more dependent on society than do the utilitarians. Human beings need a social medium in which to develop their moral potentialities. According to Green, there is a "self-realizing principle" in man. "By a consciously self-realizing principle is meant a principle that is determined to action by the conception of its own perfection, or by the idea of giving reality to possibilities which are in-

3 John Stuart Mill, *On Liberty*, p. 52.

volved in it and of which it is conscious as so involved." [4]
For men so endowed, society and government cannot be mere
instrumentalities by means of which they are better able to
satisfy their desires.   Men are interdependent with one
another for the realization of their natures.

The foundation of morality . . . in the reason or self-objectifying
consciousness of man, is the same thing as its foundation in the
institutions of a common life—in these as directed to a common
good, and so directed not mechanically but with consciousness
of the good on the part of those subject to the institutions. Such
institutions are, so to speak, the form and body of reason, as
practical in men. Without them the rational or self-conscious or
moral man does not exist, nor without them can any being have
existed from whom such a man could be developed, if any con-
tinuity of nature is implied in development.[5]

This conception of man's social dependence goes beyond
anything envisaged by the utilitarians.   Man's "self-realizing principle" has its "foundation in the institutions of a
common life."   This is to say that man is dependent on a
social environment for the emergence and realization of his
distinctively moral capacities.   Man needs society to become
what he has it in him to become.

On the basis of this theory of human nature and dynamics,
Green conceives of the function of the state in a quite different way from the utilitarians.   The state cannot be merely a
device to control men's behavior.   Rather its essential function is to release man's self-realizing principle—that is to
say, make possible his moral development—by hindering
hindrances to the achievement of the common good.   According to Green,

Our modern legislation . . . with reference to labour, and education, and health, involving as it does manifold interference
with freedom of contract, is justified on the ground that it is

---

[4] Green, *Lectures on the Principles of Political Obligation*, p. 20.
[5] Green, *Prolegomena to Ethics*, p. 216.

the business of the state, not indeed directly to promote moral goodness, for that, from the very nature of moral goodness, it cannot do, but to maintain the conditions without which a free exercise of the human faculties is impossible.[6]

Although Green does not necessarily envisage more extensive governmental interference in social and economic processes than can be justified in terms of the utilitarians' principle of utility,[7] he differs from them on the purpose of the intervention. For Green, the purpose must always be the release of men's moral potentialities, while, as John Plamenatz says, "the utilitarians share with Hobbes a complete indifference to the notion of self improvement as a thing desirable for its own sake."[8]

The revolt against classical liberal doctrine initiated by Green was carried further and given some new directions by Bernard Bosanquet. Central to Bosanquet's political theory is the idea of a general will in the sense of the direction of movement of a system of interlocking social institutions and ideas. Green had referred to "that impalpable congeries of the hopes and fears of a people, bound together by common interests and sympathy, which we call the general will."[9] He thought of the general will as a "will for the state" based on men's recognition of the usefulness of the state in promoting

[6] Green, "Liberal Legislation and Freedom of Contract," in *Works of Thomas Hill Green*, III, 374.

[7] Adam B. Ulam says that Green's "ideas on social and economic questions of the day went beyond those of the old-fashioned liberalism. He was, as English political terminology of those times went, a radical with strong ideas about the duty of the state to interfere with individual freedom wherever social needs warranted it" (*Philosophical Foundations of English Socialism*, pp. 27-28). But when we consider that the utilitarians thought of the limits of state intervention in terms of the pain that the control caused the individual and the likelihood that intervention would be wrongly made, and that Green thinks of them in terms of the effect of intervention on the individual's will to moral development, it may well be the case, in certain circumstances, that Green's theory allows a less extensive intervention than theirs.

[8] Plamenatz, *The English Utilitarians*, p. 11.

[9] Green, *Principles of Political Obligation*, p. 98.

the common good. Bosanquet's conception of the general will involves rather more than this. In particular, it involves a way of looking at man's dependence on his social environment which is significantly different from that of Green.

Bosanquet would agree with Green that man is dependent on his society for the emergence and realization of his moral potentialities. But he denies that man has either the capacity or the need for understanding his environment. Bosanquet says, "On the whole we are to the structure of legal, political, and economic organization like coral insects to a coral reef." [10]   Here Bosanquet parts company with Green. For what he does in his theory of the general will is to attribute to social processes an intrinsic rationality. In effect, he revives the classical liberals' postulate of a natural social harmony. His theory of the general will is not so much a theory of a deliberative state as of an automatic state.

Bosanquet's theory of the general will is based on his view of the nature of man's psychological processes. He says, "Neither the mind nor the community, as working organizations, can be accounted for on the principle of mere association." [11]   For Bosanquet, the doctrine of associationism does not provide a complete explanation of intellectual processes. The mind organizes its contents in a more complex way than this doctrine would allow. "In mind, as in the external world, the higher state of association is organization. The characteristic of organization is control by a general scheme as opposed to influence by juxtaposition of units." [12]   Behind this view of how the mind functions is the psychological concept of the appercipient mass. This concept is the key to Bosanquet's theory of the general will.

10 Bernard Bosanquet, "The Reality of the General Will," *International Journal of Ethics*, IV (April, 1894), 317.
11 Bosanquet, *The Philosophical Theory of the State*, p. 158.
12 *Ibid.*, p. 152.

According to Bosanquet, "The psychical elements which form the contents of the mind are so grouped and interconnected as to constitute what are technically known as Appercipient masses or systems." [13]   These masses are the ideas in terms of which a person has organized and organizes his social experience.   Common experience produces in the minds of men similar appercipient masses.   It is this similarity in the organization of the contents of their minds that is the psychological prerequisite for the existence of a general will.   "Not only may the systems of appercipient masses be *compared* to organizations of persons; they actually constitute their common mind and will.   To say that certain persons have common interests means that in this or that respect their minds are similarly or correlatively organized, that they will react in the same or correlative ways upon given presentations.   It is this identity of mental organization which is the psychological justification for the doctrine of the General Will." [14]

Of special interest is that Bosanquet regards appercipient masses as being dominant in the mind in succession.   As one comes into the individual's focus of attention, it tends to displace all the others in his consciousness.   With reference to the "psychological tendency for the activity of one appercipient system to obstruct the activity of all others," Bosanquet asserts: "It is hardly necessary to point out that, partly for this reason, though the mind must be an actual structure of systems, it is very far from being a rational system of systems.   The fact that, when one system is active, all others, as a rule, are inert, conceals the contradictions which underlie the entire fabric, and protect them from criticism and correction." [15]   What this obstructive relationship of the appercipient masses to one another implies is that no individual can fully grasp the nature of the social

13 Bosanquet, *Psychology of the Moral Self,* pp. 41-42.
14 *Ibid.,* p. 43.
15 Bosanquet, *The Philosophical Theory of the State,* p. 162.

processes in which he participates. His mind's capacity for understanding them is inherently limited by the way it functions.

But Bosanquet does think the individual rational in that his mind does attempt, partly unconsciously, to make its systems of appercipient masses a consistent system. What the individual's limitations imply is that the process of making consistent the systems of appercipient masses is essentially social. Consistency in social ideals emerges gradually in individual minds through interaction of individuals rather than through any person's total intellectual grasp of its requirements. Hence movement of a society towards consistency in its ideals is of the very essence of the general will in operation. This is to say that social processes are largely self-adjusting, for "the general will is only in part self-conscious." [16]

This will, or moving process of adjustment of ideas and institutions, Bosanquet regards as the will of the state. He conceives of the state "as the operative criticism of all institutions—the modification and adjustment by which they are capable of playing a rational part in the object of human will." [17] This statement should not be interpreted to mean that Bosanquet advocates governmental interference in social and economic processes on a large scale. He refers to "the true character of the State as a source of pervading adjustments and an idea-force holding together a complex hierarchy of groups, and not itself a separable thing like the monarch, or the 'government,' or the local body, with which we are tempted to identify it." [18] In Bosanquet's political theory the "state" is essentially an "idea-force." By this he means that it is the focus of the total system of largely self-

16 Bosanquet, "The Reality of the General Will," *International Journal of Ethics*, IV (April, 1894), 317.
17 Bosanquet, *The Philosophical Theory of the State*, p. 140.
18 *Ibid.*, pp. xxviii-xxix.

adjusting social processes. Indeed, it might be said that for Bosanquet the state is nothing less than the institutional expression in individuals' minds of the idea of consistency itself. Its psychological foundation is the rational tendency of the human mind, the tendency to seek consistency in its systems of appercipient masses.

Bosanquet does not deny, of course, that discussion and deliberation have a role to play in the process of adjustment of ideas and institutions, which is for him the general will in operation. But, and this is the significant point, it is a necessary implication of his psychological theory that these cannot play the decisive role in the expression of the general will. This is reserved to social practices; that is to say, the general will emerges through the interaction of individuals and is never entirely present to their consciousness.

It is true that Bosanquet's use of the concept of appercipient mass allows greater scope to social insight and understanding than does a psychology based on the doctrine of associationism alone. Nevertheless, his psychological theory does root man in his social environment in the sense that his understanding of social processes is necessarily limited. Man's social experience is organized rather than merely connected as in the association psychology. But the very way in which it is organized places a limit on man's capacity to understand it. What is decisive, then, for existence of a general will is that men have "unity of experience" so that their minds will be "correlatively organized." As Bosanquet puts it, "The community which organizes itself as a state will be for every group the largest body which possesses the unity of experience necessary for constituting a general will." [19]

Interlocking appercipient masses in the minds of men de-

[19] Bosanquet, "The Function of the State in Promoting the Unity of Mankind," *Proceedings of the Aristotelian Society* (New Series), XVII (1916-17), 28.

velop as a result of their common experience and provide the basis on which society moves toward a more rational life. "In practical organization, ideas adjust themselves to each other without consciousness of anything beyond an immediate daily purpose, and it is only after a long interval that people wake up and find perhaps the entire relations of classes and of industry changed as it were in their sleep." [20] If it is true to say that for Bosanquet men do not fully understand their society, it must also be said that they do not really need to understand it. For the nature of their minds is such that the social processes in which they participate are largely self-adjusting—that is to say, automatic in the sense that they need not be consciously understood by the men who carry them on. These processes are guided less by men's deliberation than by their active but unconscious reason, which manifests itself in the cumulative rationality of social practices and institutions.

In the work of A. D. Lindsay, the theory of the deliberative state takes form as a reaction against Bosanquet's theory of the general will. Lindsay says that Bosanquet's general will "can be called . . . a machine, or an organization of life." [21] It involves a mechanistic conception of society from which the purposive aspect of men's activity is excluded, and unduly depreciates men's capacity to grasp and control the consequences of their actions. According to Lindsay:

A society becomes political when the actions of its members are determined not only by this or that individual purpose but by a consciousness of the effect of their action upon the whole of society. This is something which cannot be done without conscious organization, and can be done thoroughly only by a common consciousness using the most developed political

20 Bosanquet, "The Reality of the General Will," *International Journal of Ethics*, IV (April, 1894), 318.
21 A. D. Lindsay and H. J. Laski, "Symposium: Bosanquet's Theory of the General Will," in *Mind, Matter and Purpose*, p. 32.

machinery, by an elaborate bringing to bear of the accumulated knowledge of the past and the best presaging of the future on the individual who for himself would be incapable of any such vision.   No existing society, of course, attains this ideal completely.   We find societies exhibiting different degrees of consciousness and common purposive action, but it is only as they do attain it to some extent that they get free from the control of blind economic forces.[22]

Lindsay returns to Green's conception of a consciously held common good.   From Lindsay's standpoint, Bosanquet's theory of the general will relies too heavily on social tradition and custom for guidance of men in society.   A truly political society is one in which men are much more aware of the implications of their actions.   They must be so, if they are not to be at the mercy of blind social and economic processes.   Thus Lindsay calls for a much higher degree of social understanding on the part of men than Bosanquet's psychology permits.   He sees society potentially a purposive rather than a mechanical organization of men.

A society becomes purposive through its members' becoming more aware of the ways in which the function of each is related to those of others.   The key to deepened awareness is discussion.   Lindsay says:

We are becoming increasingly to recognize that democracy can be made a reality on a large scale in so far as each member of society not only has a specific function in society but can become conscious of the relation of that function to society as a whole, and can somehow make his contribution to the general deliberations of society.   The test of democratic machinery in this view is the extent to which it makes discussion a reality and enables each member of society to make his contribution tell.[23]

22 A. D. Lindsay, in Lindsay, W. R. Sorley and Bernard Bosanquet, "Symposium: Purpose and Mechanism," *Proceedings of the Aristotelian Society* (New Series), XII (1911-12), 239-40.
23 Lindsay, "Symposium: Bosanquet's Theory of the General Will," in *Mind, Matter and Purpose*, pp. 43-44.

Here we see how the theory of the deliberative state emerges from the rejection of Bosanquet's view that society can run on the basis of each individual's performance of his function without understanding its interconnections with those of others. This is not sufficient to attain social harmony. For this, the individual must understand his relation to society as a whole and bring this understanding to bear in political deliberation.

This criticism of Bosanquet's political theory is based on Lindsay's psychological theory combined with his repudiation of the idea of automatic social harmony. He says, "Society cannot be looked upon as an aggregate of individuals, as though individuals existed first with all their nature complete and then by coming together and cooperating in various ways made the State and other communities." [24] On the point of man's social dependence, Lindsay aligns himself with Green and Bosanquet against the utilitarians. But he does not envisage social dependence in the way that Bosanquet does. Man is no "coral insect" engaged in mechanical processes but rather a moral being who needs, therefore, to control the impact of his activities on the welfare of others. Essential to this control is the association called the state.

Lindsay's view of the state is summarized in the following passage:

The State is *necessary,* not because men are selfish, but because their sympathy and interests and insight are limited as the effects of their actions are not. It is *possible* in so far as men recognize that they have obligations to other men which do not depend on the limitations or caprices of their sympathies and common interests, and in so far as they can come to know from experience what the effects of their actions are upon other men, and how by acting differently they can alter these effects.[25]

[24] Lindsay, "The State in Recent Political Theory," *The Political Quarterly,* No. 1 (Feb. 1914), p. 128.
[25] *Ibid.,* p. 139.

Here Lindsay rejects the classical liberal view that the state is a device the purpose of which is control of men's selfish tendencies. He sees it rather as being grounded in their capacity for moral purpose. At the same time, it can enable them to overcome their moral and intellectual limitations. This aspect of Lindsay's political theory links him to Bosanquet. But it is important to note that Lindsay does not find man's limitations inherent in his psychological organization and processes, as Bosanquet does, but thinks of them as limitations that arise from his relation to a complex social environment. For that environment is such that the effects of men's actions inevitably reach beyond their limited intentions. Experience shows that these effects are not always beneficent. One cannot presume the existence of any automatic social harmony. Lindsay says:

We know how tragically mistaken was the view of Bentham that if each man was allowed to pursue his own happiness the general result would be the happiness of all. Rather because men's individual actions are performed for limited ends, with limited insight, the general result of a purely individualist system would be one which no one has willed and which all might regard with loathing and despair.[26]

The state is thus for Lindsay essentially an organization through which fundamentally moral men attempt to overcome their moral and intellectual limitations in the face of partially blind social processes. There is nothing about man's psychological organization which renders this task impossible for him to accomplish. He can enlarge his understanding of how society works and take measures necessary to achieve harmony between individuals' purposes. Moreover, in taking thought about their society, men give rise to social will and purpose in themselves. Lindsay says, "The

[26] *Ibid.*, p. 140. Note also his statement: "Nineteenth-century experience has taught us that this spontaneous life of society, if left to itself, produces disastrous results, that it needs constant state control and interference" ("The State and Society," in *The International Crisis: The Theory of the State,* p. 96).

process of discovering what may be called the will of the society is a process of making it, and to that process discussion is essential." [27]   And, "The purpose of discussion is to achieve a real unity of purpose out of differences." [28]

Lindsay's restatement of the theory of the general will presents it as no automatic movement toward harmony of social ideals and institutions. Rather, it is the process of deliberately creating common social purposes out of the discordant individual purposes of limited but morally ambitious men. Given men's nature and their interdependence, the only possible way they can create and sustain social harmony is through mutual understanding combined with willingness to accommodate their separate purposes in the light of the implications of these purposes. Society cannot rely on interlocking attitudes created by unity of experience for the achievement of harmony. No doubt this helps, but experience shows that, alone, it is insufficient. Harmony depends on reason, not as an inarticulate tendency of the human mind, but as deliberately organized and applied to the analysis and control of social processes through government.

We have traced the emergence of the idea of the deliberative state in the work of Green, Bosanquet, and Lindsay. Since each built on the work of his predecessor, it has been easy to display the logic behind the evolution of modern from classical liberalism. First, the associationistic psychology was discarded for a view of man which makes him far more dependent on his society for the development of his innermost properties. But he is not seen as a dynamically empty creature. He is endowed with a "self-realizing principle," with a reason that is integral to his will. In consequence he seeks to achieve consistency in the attitudes generated by his social experience. Then the assumption of an automatic social harmony which persisted through the

[27] Lindsay, *The Essentials of Democracy*, p. 40.
[28] *Ibid.*, p. 41.

work of Bosanquet was called into question. Man's innate but inarticulate rationality does not ensure that society will move toward greater consistency and harmony in its ideals and institutions. Experience suggests the contrary. Only through discussion and deliberation can the requirements of justice and the general welfare be discovered and fulfilled.

It would not do, however, to overstate the differences between classical and modern liberalism. As we have seen, there are elements of both doctrines in the work of John Stuart Mill. Lindsay says of the utilitarians that "the central inconsistency in their doctrine, that they sometimes wrote as if men's interests were naturally harmonious, sometimes as if they had to be artificially harmonized, came from their soundly if unconsciously recognizing that both those things are always true." [29] In this perspective, it would be true to say that in the liberal view the function of the state has always been, as Lindsay puts it, "to make the Community more of a Community." [30] Where the liberal doctrines differ is over the ways in which it is proposed that the state perform this function. If modern liberalism thinks of these in terms of calculated adjustments arising from deliberation rather than in terms of indoctrination and legal constraint, it is because it holds a view of man and his relation to society different from that of classical liberalism. To the modern liberal, man is more rational and social processes are less rational than the classical liberal had thought.

Now that we have seen how modern liberalism has come to differ from classical liberalism and why it is that a modern liberal such as Lindsay regards discussion as the essence of the democratic process, we must ask whether his views are typical of modern liberal thinking. The answer to this question is yes. For if we consider the work of others, although we find differences in detail and in emphasis, the

29 Lindsay, *The Modern Democratic State*, I, 145.
30 *Ibid.*, p. 245.

main line of thinking about man and the state is the same
as Lindsay's.   For example, Ernest Barker says, "We cannot
make a distinction between the sovereignty of the idea of
justice and the sovereignty of social thought.   The two are
inseparable.   There is no justice but social thinking makes
it so; and conversely there is no social thinking about the
order of human relations but issues in the idea of justice." [31]
In Barker's work the modern liberal view of the primacy of
discussion is given an extended temporal setting.   He sees
man as an ambivalent but fundamentally moral creature
whose nature forces him to reflect upon the kind of society
that will best meet his various needs.[32]   In this connection,
Barker emphasizes the contribution which the party system
makes toward organizing and focusing discussion.   By way
of further example, we may point to the statement of J.
Roland Pennock that the "essence of democratic procedure
is not the counting of heads or even the obtaining of consent.
Rather it is the processes of discussion, adjustment, and co-
operative activity." [33]   Pennock sees man as an ambivalent
yet predominantly social creature endowed with moral purpose.   He contends that "Man's social nature requires the
indefinite extension of equal rights for its satisfaction." [34]
He contemplates the possibility of consiliency and harmony
of human interests.   But this social harmony is not seen as
arising in any purely spontaneous fashion.   Rather it can
only be achieved through democratic processes.

Barker and Pennock are in agreement with the essentials
of Lindsay's psychological and political theory.   There is
plenty of room for difference in modern liberal doctrine
about the relative contributions of specific items of political
machinery to the fulfillment of human purposes.   But on
the score of men's need for an organized and elaborate

[31] Barker, *Principles of Social & Political Theory*, pp. 214-15.
[32] *Ibid.*, pp. 273ff.
[33] Pennock, *Liberal Democracy: Its Merits and Prospects*, p. 280.
[34] *Ibid.*, p. 93.

system of discussion to generate mutual understanding and appreciation of the requirements of the "common life," there is consensus among modern liberals. That this is the case should occasion no surprise. As De Ruggiero says, "Liberalism is conscious that the formation of human individualities is the work of freedom. No demand of the higher life can be effectually made, unless it is made spontaneously by the spirit; no progress will be enduringly achieved, unless it is a conscious development from within." [35] Modern liberalism has left the doctrines of associationism and a self-regulating society behind. Rational and moral action is not the fruit of indoctrination, as James Mill would have it. Rather it is the product of the release of individuality, and to this, free deliberation is essential.

In comparing Rousseau's theory of the general will with the theory of the deliberative state, it is well to keep in mind Charles William Hendel's observation that "the genius of Rousseau was pre-eminently psychological." [36] When set beside the complexity of his psychological theory, Rousseau's political theory appears almost incongruously crude. "Rousseau," says Lindsay, "is the worst of guides to the practical realization of his own ideal." [37] Any exponent of the deliberative state envisages a system of social and political institutions in comparison with which Rousseau's conception of the political machine seems a drastic oversimplification. He did not entirely disregard all that partial focusing of public opinion which the modern liberal sees taking place in private associations. But for him the general will is primarily a political concept. Its locus is the state, not society where the modern liberal tends to place it. Moreover, Rousseau was unaware of the possibility of a party system, which plays so large a role in modern liberal thought.

35 Guido de Ruggiero, *The History of European Liberalism*, p. 358.
36 Hendel, *Jean-Jacques Rousseau: Moralist*, I, 73.
37 A. D. Lindsay, *Karl Marx's Capital: An Introductory Essay*, p. 111.

He thinks of the desirability of small states. Some echos of this may be heard in modern liberal thinking,[38] but no modern liberal seriously considers it.

It is true that Rousseau wrote before technical progress enabled democratic government to be carried on over much larger areas than in the past. The deliberative state, as we know it, is possible only on the basis of the scope and rapidity of modern means of communication. Nevertheless, Rousseau's capacity for political invention was clearly limited. It broke down completely, as we have seen, in his effort to solve the problem of how to keep government responsive to the general will. The best he could do was to recommend the device of the periodical assembly, hallowed in his eyes by Roman practice; and to insure its effectiveness, he was led to advocate the totalitarian idea of a civil religion. Here Rousseau's faith in the liberated reason of men faltered, and he sought to achieve liberal ends by authoritarian means.

In analytical terms, Rousseau's theory of human nature and dynamics may be regarded as a synthesis of the views of Hobbes and Locke, in which the principle of transformation partially replaces the principle of association as an explanation of man's relation to his social environment. Because of this principle of transformation in his view of man, Rousseau's political theory differs markedly from the classical liberal democratic pattern of thought. Human dynamics do include associative processes. On this point, Rousseau and the classical liberals are in agreement. But exclusive reliance on these processes involves for Rousseau, as it does not for the classical liberals, violation of man's moral potentialities. It means achievement of the appearance, at the expense of the substance, of moral ideals, utilitarian behavior without moral freedom. Rousseau's patriotic citizen

---

38 Note Lindsay's statement: "The discrepancy between the area of government dictated by the capacity for good governing and the area dictated by the need for government is one of the most baffling disharmonies of politics, and is with us all" (*The Essentials of Democracy*, p. 20).

is not James Mill's economic man, but both are creatures of association, lacking insight and individuality.

Rousseau's differences from classical liberalism relate him to modern liberalism. The modern liberal shares with Rousseau a conception of man's social dependence that goes beyond anything found in classical liberal doctrine. The reason is that both think of man as a creature with potentialities that may develop only in an appropriate social medium. There is "nature" within him; he has a "self-realizing principle" that his society may either thwart or fulfil. Social and political institutions must take account of man's autonomous tendencies.

In addition, both the modern liberal and Rousseau think of man as ambivalent, although for Rousseau ambivalence approaches contradictoriness when the strain of psychological hedonism is uppermost in his thinking. He conceives of human ambivalence as a conflict between productive and egoistic tendencies. The former are rooted in man's reason and conscience, while the latter appear as bias in favor of his personal good, which impairs his capacity for moral deliberation and action. A modern liberal such as Lindsay thinks of man as a being who recognizes the existence of obligations to his fellows, but whose moral and intellectual limitations prevent him from fully meeting these obligations without the aid of elaborate institutional supports. But no difference in principle of a substantial kind is involved here. Both Lindsay and Rousseau think of the state as essentially the institutional expression of man's moral purpose, which purpose includes recognition of an obligation to neutralize his selfish tendencies and their effects. For them, the state is the means by which man releases his moral potential and seeks to realize goodness and justice; it is not merely a device by which men are enabled to control one another. Neither pictures man as the egoistic yet plastic creature of the utilitarians. Both see man's need for liberty in his capacity for moral growth, in his "perfectibility," as Rousseau would say. These ideas about man and the state which relate Rousseau to modern liberalism also differentiate them both from classical liberalism.

Rousseau and modern liberals also agree in principle on how to achieve social harmony. The general will may be expressed only through deliberation of the people. Above all others, this idea connects Rousseau's thought to the theory of the deliberative state. It is true that Rousseau's formulation of it is a vast oversimplification of the polititcal process. "If, when the people, being furnished with adequate information, held its deliberations, the citizens had no communication one with another, the grand total of small differences would always give the general will, and the decision would always be good." [39] On the basis of this formula for expression of the general will, Rousseau, by assuming that the people are sufficiently informed, all but assumes away the political problem as the modern liberal sees it. Social processes are apt to be blind precisely because people are not sufficiently informed as to the implications of their ideas and actions. Part of the purpose of discussion is to enhance their awareness of these. Much of the administrative machinery of government is devoted to their analysis. But this qualification does not vitiate the point that on the principle of discussion as the way to transcend the biases of individuals, Rousseau and modern liberals stand together.

The difference between them is on the source of these biases. Rousseau is thinking primarily in terms of the necessity for overcoming distortions in individuals' judgments on the requirements of justice and the general welfare. It is the intrinsic fallibility of man's judgment based on his propensity to rationalize and his tendency to seek his personal good without regard for that of others that concern

[39] Rousseau, *The Social Contract*, Book II, ch. 3.

Rousseau, and for which he sees a remedy in the joint effort of group deliberation. The modern liberal, however, is thinking primarily of discussion as a means for discovering and eliminating destructive consequences of partially blind social and economic processes. For the modern liberal, it is not only the limitations of man's moral nature, but also the nature of his society, that make discussion the imperative of the democratic process. But both the theory of the general will and the theory of the deliberative state seek to enhance the role of reason in human life. Unlike Bosanquet and the philosophers of the Enlightenment, neither Rousseau nor modern liberals assume the existence of a movement toward social harmony immanent in historical and economic processes. For them, in Lindsay's words, a truly political society is a "purposive society." [40]

Finally, we observe that both Rousseau and the modern liberals repudiate the atomism of classical liberal democratic theory. But for neither does man's social dependence involve sacrifice of his individuality. Modern liberalism is concerned with the problem of community and the promotion of what Lindsay calls a "common life." This conception requires not depreciation but rather maximization of individuality. As Carleton Kemp Allen puts it:

The notion that the man who values, guards, and cultivates his own individuality is setting himself in opposition to the interest of society is a profound misunderstanding. It is the essence of democracy that the public interest cannot flourish without the cultivation of the individual's interest in himself. The Together-Will must be the aggregation of real and vigorous individual wills; otherwise it becomes that devouring monster, mass emotion, goaded by unconscionable and overweening individual will.[41]

[40] Lindsay, "Symposium: Purpose and Mechanism," *Proceedings of the Aristotelian Society* (New Series), XII (1911-12), 239.
[41] Allen, *Democracy and the Individual*, p. 105.

This view of the relation between community and individuality is of the essence of Rousseau's theory of the general will. He is concerned for man's moral autonomy as well as his political freedom, for his capacity to make his own appraisals of values and to be independent. These are the prerequisites to his attaining an appropriate relation to society and to the expression of the general will. Here is no atomistic theory of man's relation to society. Rather it is a theory which, while giving full weight to man's dependence on his society, sees in him capacities for autonomy and responsibility and demands that he exercise them.

Despite his deviations from this ideal—and notably so in his proposals for intensification of social sentiment—individual autonomy is the key to Rousseau's moral and political theory. Human dynamics are such that without independence men remain slaves of their socially accentuated egoistic tendencies. Their moral potentialities lie dormant, and society drifts toward prideful materialism. This drift may be defeated either by their achievement of moral freedom or by their indoctrination with patriotism combined with devotion to justice and the general welfare. Only the first involves no violation of man's nature as Rousseau discerns it, of man's capacity for moral creativity. The latter destroys this capacity.

William Ernest Hocking once said the liberal spirit "is human nature's revolt against its perpetual tendency to egoism." [42] This is the spirit which moves in Rousseau's work.

[42] Hocking, *The Lasting Elements of Individualism*, p. 38.

LIST OF WORKS
CITED

Allen, Carleton Kemp. Democracy and the Individual. London: Oxford University Press, 1943.

Aristotle. Politics. Translated with notes by Ernest Barker. Oxford: Clarendon Press, 1948.

Asch, Solomon E. Social Psychology. New York: Prentice-Hall, 1952.

Ashton, T. S. The Industrial Revolution, 1760-1830. London: Oxford University Press, 1948.

Babbitt, Irving. Rousseau and Romanticism. Boston: Houghton, Mifflin, 1919.

Barker, Ernest. Principles of Social and Political Theory. Oxford: Clarendon Press, 1951.

Barzun, Jacques. Romanticism and the Modern Ego. Boston: Little, Brown, 1943.

Becker, Carl L. The Heavenly City of the Eighteenth-Century Philosophers. New Haven: Yale University Press, 1932.

Bentham, Jeremy. A Fragment on Government and An Introduction to the Principles of Morals and Legislation. Edited with an introduction by Wilfrid Harrison. Oxford: Basil Blackwell, 1948. "Blackwell's Political Texts."

Bosanquet, Bernard. "The Function of the State in Promoting the Unity of Mankind," Proceedings of the Aristotelian Society (New Series), XVII (1916-17), 28-57.

——The Philosophical Theory of the State. 4th ed. London: Macmillan, 1951.

——Psychology of the Moral Self. London: Macmillan, 1904.

——"The Reality of the General Will," *International Journal of Ethics,* IV (April, 1894), 308-20.

Bouchardy, François. "Une Définition de la conscience par J.-J. Rousseau," *Annales de la Société Jean-Jacques Rousseau,* XXXII (1950-52), 167-75.

Bowle, John. Western Political Thought: An Historical Introduction from the Origins to Rousseau. New York: Oxford University Press, 1948.

Boyd, William. The Educational Theory of Jean Jacques Rousseau. London: Longmans, Green, 1911.

Brandt, Richard B. Hopi Ethics: A Theoretical Analysis. Chicago: University of Chicago Press, 1954.

Bury, J. B. The Idea of Progress: An Inquiry into its Origin and Growth. London: Macmillan, 1928.

Carritt, E. F. Morals and Politics: Theories of Their Relation from Hobbes and Spinoza to Marx and Bosanquet. London: Oxford University Press, 1935.

Cassirer, Ernst. The Philosophy of the Enlightenment. Translated by Fritz C. A. Koelln and James P. Pettegrove. Princeton: Princeton University Press, 1951.

——The Question of Jean-Jacques Rousseau. Translated and edited with an introduction and additional notes by Peter Gay. New York: Columbia University Press, 1954.

Cobban, Alfred. The Crisis of Civilization. London: J. Cape [1941].

——Rousseau and the Modern State. London: George Allen & Unwin, 1934.

Cole, G. D. H. "Rousseau's Political Theory," in G. D. H. Cole, Essays in Social Theory. London: Macmillan, 1950.

——"Rousseau's *Social Contract,*" in G. D. H. Cole, Persons and Periods: Studies. London: Macmillan, 1938.

Collingwood, R. G. The Idea of Nature. Oxford: Clarendon Press, 1945.

Cooley, Charles Horton. Human Nature and the Social Order. New York: Scribners, 1902.

Cranston, Maurice. Freedom: A New Analysis. London: Longmans, Green, 1953.

Derathé, Robert. Le Rationalisme de J.-J. Rousseau. Paris: Presses Universitaires de France, 1948. "Bibliothèque de philosophie contemporaine."

Frankel, Charles. The Faith of Reason: The Idea of Progress in the French Enlightenment. New York: King's Crown Press, 1948.

Gide, Charles, and Charles Rist. A History of Economic Doctrines, from the Time of the Physiocrats to the Present Day. Translated by R. Richards. 2d Eng. ed. London: Harrap, 1949.

Gierke, Otto. Natural Law and the Theory of Society, 1500-1800. Translated with an introduction by Ernest Barker. 2 vols. Cambridge: The University Press, 1934.

Girvetz, Harry K. From Wealth to Welfare: The Evolution of Liberalism. Stanford: Stanford University Press, 1950.

Gough, J. W. John Locke's Political Philosophy: Eight Studies. Oxford: Clarendon Press, 1950.

Green, Thomas Hill. Lectures on the Principles of Political Obligation. Introduction by Lord Lindsay. London: Longmans, Green, 1941.

——"Liberal Legislation and Freedom of Contract," in Vol. III of Works of Thomas Hill Green, edited by R. L. Nettleship. London: Longmans, Green, 1906.

——Prolegomena to Ethics. Edited by A. C. Bradley. 2d ed. Oxford: Clarendon Press, 1884.

Groethuysen, Bernard. Jean-Jacques Rousseau. Paris: Gallimard, 1949.

Halévy, Elie. The Growth of Philosophic Radicalism. Translated by Mary Morris. Preface by A. D. Lindsay. New York: Augustus M. Kelly, 1949.

Hallowell, John H. Main Currents in Modern Political Thought. New York: Holt, 1950.

Hendel, Charles William. Jean-Jacques Rousseau: Moralist. 2 vols. London: Oxford University Press, 1934.

Hobbes, Thomas. Leviathan. Edited with an introduction by Michael Oakeshott. Oxford: Basil Blackwell, n.d. "Blackwell's Political Texts."

Hocking, William Ernest. Human Nature and Its Remaking. New Haven: Yale University Press, 1918.

——The Lasting Elements of Individualism. New Haven: Yale University Press, 1937.

——Man and the State. New Haven: Yale University Press, 1926.

Kendall, Willmoore. John Locke and the Doctrine of Majority Rule. Urbana: University of Illinois Press, 1941.

Knight, Frank H. "Ethics and Economic Reform," in Frank H. Knight, Freedom and Reform: Essays in Economics and Social Philosophy. New York: Harper, 1947.

Krech, David, and Richard S. Crutchfield. Theory and Problems of Social Psychology. New York: McGraw-Hill, 1948.

Lamprecht, Sterling Power. The Moral and Political Philosophy of John Locke. New York: Columbia University Press, 1918.

Laski, Harold J. The Rise of Liberalism: The Philosophy of a Business Civilization. New York: Harper, 1936.

Lefebvre, Georges. The Coming of the French Revolution. Translated by R. R. Palmer. Princeton: Princeton University Press, 1947.

Lindsay, A. D. The Essentials of Democracy. 2d ed. London: Oxford University Press, 1951.

——Karl Marx's Capital: An Introductory Essay. London: Oxford University Press, 1925.

——The Modern Democratic State, Vol. I. New York: Oxford University Press, 1947.

——"The State and Society," in The International Crisis: The Theory of the State. London: Oxford University Press, 1916.

——"The State in Recent Political Theory," *The Political Quarterly,* No. 1 (February, 1914), pp. 128-45.

Lindsay, A. D., and H. J. Laski. "Symposium: Bosanquet's Theory of the General Will," in Mind, Matter and Purpose. London: Harrison and Sons, 1928. Aristotelian Society, Supplementary Volume III.

Lindsay, A. D., W. R. Sorley, and Bernard Bosanquet. "Symposium: Purpose and Mechanism," *Proceedings of the Aristotelian Society* (New Series), XII (1911-12), 216-63.

Locke, John. An Essay Concerning Human Understanding. New ed. London: George Routledge and Sons, n.d.

Machiavelli, Niccolò. The Prince and The Discourses. Introduction by Max Lerner. New York: The Modern Library, 1950.

MacIver, Robert M. The Ramparts We Guard. New York: Macmillan, 1950.

——Society: A Textbook of Sociology. New York: Rinehart, 1948.

——The Web of Government. New York: Macmillan, 1947.

Macpherson, C. B. "The Social Bearing of Locke's Political Theory," *The Western Political Quarterly*, VII (March, 1954), 1-22.

Mill, James. Analysis of the Phenomena of the Human Mind. New ed. 2 vols. London: Longmans, Green, Reader, and Dyer, 1869.

——An Essay on Government. Introduction by Ernest Barker. Cambridge: The University Press, 1937.

Mill, John Stuart. On Liberty and Considerations on Representative Government. Edited with an introduction by R. B. McCallum. Oxford: Basil Blackwell, 1947.

——Principles of Political Economy, with Some of Their Applications to Social Philosophy. Edited with an introduction by Sir W. J. Ashley. New ed. London: Longmans, Green, 1923.

——Utilitarianism. Oxford: Basil Blackwell, 1949.

Murphy, Gardner. Historical Introduction to Modern Psychology. Rev. ed. New York: Harcourt, Brace, 1949.

Myrdal, Gunnar. "The Trend towards Economic Planning," *The Manchester School of Economic and Social Studies*, XIX (January, 1951), 1-42.

Pennock, J. Roland. Liberal Democracy: Its Merits and Prospects. New York: Rinehart, 1950.

Plamenatz, John. The English Utilitarians. Oxford: Basil Blackwell, 1949.

——The Revolutionary Movement in France, 1815-71. London: Longmans, Green, 1952.

Randall, John Herman, Jr. The Making of the Modern Mind. Rev. ed. Boston: Houghton Mifflin, 1940.

Robbins, Lionel. The Theory of Economic Policy in English Classical Political Economy. London: Macmillan, 1952.

Rose, John Holland. The Life of Napoleon I: Including New Materials from the British Official Records. 2 vols. New York: Macmillan, 1902.

Rousseau, Jean Jacques. Confessions. Translated by John Grant. 2 vols. New York: Dutton, 1931. "Everyman's Library."

——Émile. Translated by Barbara Foxley. New York: Dutton, 1948. "Everyman's Library."

——The Political Writings of Jean Jacques Rousseau. Edited by C. E. Vaughan. 2 vols. Cambridge: The University Press, 1915.

——Rousseau: Political Writings. Translated and edited by Frederick Watkins. London: Thomas Nelson and Sons, 1953.

——The Social Contract and Discourses. Translated with an introduction by G. D. H. Cole. New York: Dutton, 1950. "Everyman's Library."

Ruggiero, Guido de. The History of European Liberalism. Translated by R. G. Collingwood. London: Oxford University Press, 1927.

Russell, Bertrand. A History of Western Philosophy, and Its Connection with Political and Social Circumstances from the Earliest Times to the Present Day. New York: Simon and Schuster, 1945.

Sabine, George H. "The Two Democratic Traditions," *The Philosophical Review*, LXI (October, 1952), 451-74.

Social Contract: Essays by Locke, Hume and Rousseau. Introduction by Sir Ernest Barker. New York: Oxford University Press, 1948. "Galaxy Edition."

Strauss, Leo. Natural Right and History. Chicago: University of Chicago Press, 1953.

——The Political Philosophy of Hobbes: Its Basis and Its Genesis. Translated by Elsa M. Sinclair. Oxford: Clarendon Press, 1936.

Talmon, J. L. The Rise of Totalitarian Democracy. Boston: Beacon Press, 1952. "Beacon Studies in Freedom and Power."

Thompson, J. M. The French Revolution. New York: Oxford University Press, 1945.

Ulam, Adam B. Philosophical Foundations of English Socialism. Cambridge, Mass.: Harvard University Press, 1951. "Harvard Political Studies."

Watkins, Frederick. The Political Tradition of the West: A Study in the Development of Modern Liberalism. Cambridge, Mass.: Harvard University Press, 1948.

Western Tradition, The: A Series of Talks Given in the B. B. C. European Programme. London: Vox Mundi, 1949.

Woolf, Leonard. After the Deluge. 2 vols. New York: Harcourt, Brace, 1931, 1939.

Wright, Ernest Hunter. The Meaning of Rousseau. London: Oxford University Press, 1929.

INDEX

OF

PERSONS